Printed in Dallas, Texas by The Odee Company

Contact: contact@first15.org
www.first15.org

Designed by Matt Ravenelle
mattravenelle.com

ABOUT FIRST15

Spending time alone with God every day can be a struggle. We're busier – and more stressed – than ever. But still, we know it's important to spend time alone with our Creator. We know we need to read his word, pray, and worship him.

First15 bridges the gap between desire and reality, helping you establish the rhythm of meaningful, daily experiences in God's presence. First15 answers the critical questions:

- Why should I spend time alone with God?
- How do I spend time alone with God?
- How do I get the most out of my time alone with God?
- How can I become more consistent with my time alone with God?

And by answering these questions through the format of daily devotionals, you'll practice the rhythm of meeting with God while experiencing the incredible gift of his loving presence given to those who make time to meet with him.

Allow God's passionate pursuit to draw you in across the next several days. And watch as every day is better than the last as your life is built on the solid foundation of God's love through the power of consistent, meaningful time alone with him.

To learn more about First15, visit our website first15. org. First15 is available across mobile app, email, podcast, and our website. Subscribe to our devotional today and experience God in a fresh way every day.

———————

ABOUT THE AUTHOR

Craig Denison is the author of First15, a daily devotional guiding over a million believers into a fresh experience with God every day. In 2015, Craig founded First15 after sensing a longing in God's heart for his people to be about relationship – real, restored relationship with him – that above all else, he simply wanted the hearts of his people. Craig began praying, dreaming, and writing. And the idea of helping people spend the first fifteen minutes of their day focusing on nothing else but growing in their relationship with God was born. The vision was birthed in Craig's heart that if we as a people would worship, read, and pray at the beginning of every day, everything could change for the better. Craig writes, speaks, and he and his wife, Rachel lead worship to help believers establish a more tangible, meaningful connection with God.

———————————

CONTENTS

A foundation of love
Week 1

Love God
Week 2

Love people
Week 3

Love in action
Week 4

Day 1 - His Love Pursues Us   12-15
Day 2 - His Love Has Redeemed Us   16-19
Day 3 - His Love Has Set Us Free   20-23
Day 4 - All He Asks of Us is Love   24-27
Day 5 - The Joy of a Love-based Life   28-31
Day 6 - Love-based Obedience   32-35
Day 7 - Love-based Simplicity   36-39

Day 8 - Love God: It's All about Relationship   46-49
Day 9 - Love People   50-53
Day 10 - A Life of Sacrifice   54-57
Day 11 - Rest in God   58-61
Day 12 - The Discipline of Simplicity   62-65
Day 13 - The Simple Truth of Freedom from Sin   66-69
Day 14 - The Simplicity of Grace   70-73

Day 15 - Living without Offense   80-83
Day 16 - Seeing Past the Brokenness   84-87
Day 17 - Jesus is the Model   88-91
Day 18 - Loving Family   92-95
Day 19 - Loving Friends   96-99
Day 20 - Loving Strangers   100-103
Day 21 - Loving the Church   104-107

Day 22 - Action Fueled by Love   114-117
Day 23 - Love is Present   118-120
Day 24 - Love Makes Time for Others   122-125
Day 25 - Love Encourages   126-129
Day 26 - Love Forgives   130-133
Day 27 - Love Hopes   134-137
Day 28 - Love Wins   138-141

A foundation of love

"For I am sure that neither death nor life, nor angels nor rulers, nor things present nor things to come, nor powers, nor height nor depth, nor anything else in all creation, will be able to separate us from the love of God in Christ Jesus our Lord." Romans 8:38-39

WEEKLY OVERVIEW

1 Corinthians 13:13 says, *"So now faith, hope, and love abide, these three; but the greatest of these is love."* The greatest of all aspects of the Christian life is love. Love is to be at the foundation of all we do, all we are, and all we hold on to. If we focus on love and allow the Holy Spirit to strip everything else away, what will be left is a life of blessed simplicity rooted in face-to-face relationship with our heavenly Father. As we spend time this week looking at the simplicity of love, I pray that all the weighty, frivolous things of the world that rob you of an abundant life fall away in light of the glorious goodness of God's unconditional and wholly available love for you.

His Love Pursues Us

DEVOTIONAL

The fact that we are pursued by the Creator of the universe is an unfathomable truth perfectly illustrating the amazing love our heavenly Father has for us. Ephesians 2:8 says, *"For by grace you have been saved through faith. And this is not your own doing; it is the gift of God."* Those of us who have believed in and accepted the free gift of salvation have been lifted out of the world's foundation of works-based living and ushered into a new standard of grace. By grace

"We love because he first loved us."

alone we have wonderful, restored relationship with the God who passionately pursues us in every season of life. And by grace alone our lives are now based on the unconditional love of our good Father.

1 John 4:8 says, *"Anyone who does not love does not know God, because God is love."* All that God does is love because it is his very nature. Every word of Scripture was authored because he loves us. Every good thing we have in life is only available to us because he loves us. The fact that you and I have air in our lungs is a miraculous demonstration of God's overwhelming faithfulness. The fact that we can enter into such a depth of relationship with a perfect, holy God reveals his heart to pursue us.

Revelation 3:20 says, *"Behold, I stand at the door and knock. If anyone hears my voice and opens the door, I will come in to him and eat with him, and he with me."* This passage in Revelation is God's word to the lukewarm church in Laodicea. God doesn't just knock on the doors of hearts already filled with passion for him. He doesn't just knock on the doors of the lost. He knocks on the doors of the hearts that are in desperate need of inner revival through his tangible, powerful love. He knocks on the doors of the hearts whose flame has been squelched by the cares and stresses of this world that he might come and reignite passionate communion between our spirit and the Holy Spirit.

The God of heaven and earth is passionately pursuing you right now. No matter how close you are to him, he is knocking on the door of your heart, asking to come in and meet with you once again. He's not knocking just to fix you. He's not knocking just to make you do something for him. He simply wants to meet with you. He simply wants to love you.

How you respond to the passionate pursuit of God is totally up to you. There is grace for you today to seek the face of your heavenly Father. There is grace to open up your heart and accept the wonderful gift of encountering God's presence. There is grace to know and experience the depths of God's love for you. The question before you is simply this: will you choose today to let God love you?

GUIDED PRAYER

1. Meditate on the heart of your heavenly Father to pursue you in love.

"Can a woman forget her nursing child, that she should have no compassion on the son of her womb? Even these may forget, yet I will not forget you." Isaiah 49:15

"In this is love, not that we have loved God but that he loved us and sent his Son to be the propitiation for our sins." 1 John 4:10

"I have loved you with an everlasting love; therefore I have continued my faithfulness to you." Jeremiah 31:3

2. Open up your heart to your loving Father. Ask him to reveal his nearness and love. Ask him to reveal his presence that you might spend time truly meeting with him today.

"Behold, I stand at the door and knock. If anyone hears my voice and opens the door, I will come in to him and eat with him, and he with me." Revelation 3:20

"But from there you will seek the Lord your God and you will find him, if you search after him with all your heart and with all your soul." Deuteronomy 4:29

3. Take time to simply let God love you. Open up the places of your heart that are broken, wounded, and cause you pain. Confess any sins that are holding you back from walking in the fullness of relationship available to you. Don't move on from God's presence until you feel he has done the work he desires to do today.

Taking time to sit in the presence of God and simply receive his love is foundational to every other aspect of Christianity. All of eternity is simply about being with our Creator. It's all about allowing God to love us and giving him our hearts in return. May Ephesians 3:14-19 stir your heart to truly seek a revelatory knowledge of God's love for you:

For this reason I bow my knees before the Father, from whom every family in heaven and on earth is named, that according to the riches of his glory he may grant you to be strengthened with power through his Spirit in your inner being, so that Christ may dwell in your hearts through faith—that you, being rooted and grounded in love, may have strength to comprehend with all the saints what is the breadth and length and height and depth, and to know the love of Christ that surpasses knowledge, that you may be filled with all the fullness of God.

Extended Reading: Ephesians 2

His Love Has Redeemed Us

DAY 2

DEVOTIONAL

The eternal redemption afforded to us by the powerful sacrifice of Jesus is a wonderful, life-giving demonstration of God's unconditional, unchanging love. I've gone through much of my life feeling condemned. I look at my thoughts, actions, reactions, and failures and apply my condemning perspective to my perception of my heavenly Father. But in reality, he has so faithfully demonstrated

"For with the Lord there is steadfast love, and with him is plentiful redemption."

PSALM 130:7

his overwhelming love to me through the securing of my redemption. In reality, he truly loves me just as I am even with all my failures and faults.

Colossians 1:19-22 says,

For in him all the fullness of God was pleased to dwell, and through him to reconcile to himself all things, whether on earth or in heaven, making peace by the blood of his cross. And you, who once were alienated and hostile in mind, doing evil deeds, he has now reconciled in his body of flesh by his death, in order to present you holy and blameless and above reproach before him.

God sees you and me as *"holy and blameless."* Through his love we have been totally redeemed: set right before the God whose perspectives and beliefs are true above all else. When he says we are redeemed, that truth is now meant to be at the foundation of all we think, believe, and do.

Psalm 130:7 says, *"O Israel, hope in the Lord! For with the Lord there is steadfast love, and with him is plentiful redemption."* You and I are redeemed apart from anything we do. We are made holy

apart from any inherent ability or worthiness we possess: God's passionate desire for restored relationship with us caused him to secure what you and I could never attain on our own: the eternal redemption of all who believe in Jesus Christ.

17

So what does it mean for you to be redeemed? What effect does redemption have on your day today? 1 Peter 1:14-15 says, *"As obedient children, do not be conformed to the passions of your former ignorance, but as he who called you is holy, you also be holy in all your conduct."* Live your life today in light of the redemption secured for you by Jesus. Allow the Holy Spirit to do a mighty work and help you live differently today than you did yesterday. Your past failures and weaknesses do not define you. Your present misconceptions and sins can be forgiven, healed, and transformed this instant. Jesus made a clear path for you to live a life worthy of the calling you have received (Ephesians 4:1). All that is required of you is to believe, trust, open your heart to God, and live today in the constant communion God desires with you. May your day today be filled with the life-giving transformation and freedom that comes from living in light of your present redemption.

GUIDED PRAYER

1. Meditate on the redemption secured for you by the powerful sacrifice of Jesus.

"In him we have redemption through his blood, the forgiveness of our trespasses, according to the riches of his grace." Ephesians 1:7

"O Israel, hope in the Lord! For with the Lord there is steadfast love, and with him is plentiful redemption." Psalm 130:7

"He entered once for all into the holy places, not by means of the blood of goats and calves but by means of his own blood, thus securing an eternal redemption." Hebrews 9:12

2. Where have sins, lies, past failures, or wounds been causing you to live apart from your redemption? Where has your life looked more like the world and less like heaven? Confess those sins and your need of God's forgiveness, transformation, and presence.

"Repent therefore, and turn back, that your sins may be blotted out, that times of refreshing may come from the presence of the Lord." Acts 3:19-20

"If we confess our sins, he is faithful and just to forgive us our sins and to cleanse us from all unrighteousness." 1 John 1:9

3. Receive God's forgiveness. Spend time opening your heart and receiving his presence.

"If you, O Lord, should mark iniquities, O Lord, who could stand? But with you there is forgiveness, that you may be feared." Psalm 130:3-4

"My presence will go with you, and I will give you rest." Exodus 33:14

Our heavenly Father is wholly patient with us as we learn to live out this incredible gift of redemption. He is perfectly kind and forgiving when we come to him and confess our sin. And he has a perfect plan every day for our transformation, healing, and freedom if we will simply make space in our lives to spend time with him and receive all he has to give. May we as the body of Christ learn what it is to live in light of the glorious inheritance of redemption, freedom, and abundant life secured for us by the precious blood of Jesus.

Extended Reading: 1 Peter 1

His Love
Has Set Us Free

DEVOTIONAL

What does it look like to be totally free in Christ Jesus? What does it look like to live in the world, but be free from the constraints, demands, burdens, and stresses of living for the world? Scripture proclaims to us a life more abundant, purposeful, and free than what I am now experiencing. The Holy Spirit quietly but clearly beckons me to choose him throughout my day that I might know what it is to live in constant communion with him. God clearly has a plan for us far greater than anything we have yet experienced. And he longs for today to be a day marked by the freedom of life that only comes through a transformational encounter with his presence, truth, and love.

God's love has set us free from everything that would entangle us to this world. His love sets us free emotionally, spiritually, and practically. His love broke the chains of sin and depravity as Jesus breathed his last breath on the cross. His love broke through to earth as he tore the veil from top to bottom signifying the availability of his presence for all. His love broke through in each of our lives as we said yes to crowning him King and accepted his free gift of eternal relationship with him. And his love breaks through every morning as surely as the sun rises, declaring to us the availability of a day filled with his nearness and love.

Scripture says in Romans 7:4, *"Likewise, my brothers, you also have died to the law through the body of Christ, so that you may belong to another, to him who has been raised from the dead, in order that we may bear fruit for God."* And in Galatians 5:22-23, Scripture says, *"But the fruit of the Spirit is love, joy, peace, patience, kindness, goodness, faithfulness, gentleness, self-control; against such things there is no law."* God longs for our lives to be marked by the presence of the Holy Spirit. He longs for us to bear his fruit that we might enjoy all that restored relationship with him affords us.

Romans 8:1-3 says, *"There is therefore now no condemnation for those who are in Christ Jesus. For the law of the Spirit of life has set you free in Christ Jesus from the law of sin and death. For God has done what the law, weakened by the flesh, could not do."* God's love has set us free from "the law of sin and death" that we might live by the law of *"the Spirit of life."* His love has made a way for us to be fully known and fully loved. But the choice is still ours today. Will we submit ourselves to this new law marked by the fruit of his presence, or will we choose to resubmit ourselves to the law of this world as if the death of Christ was for nothing? Choose abundant life today by opening your heart and experiencing the nearness of the Holy Spirit.

GUIDED PRAYER

1. Meditate on the freedom of life available to you through Christ. Allow Scripture to stir up your faith and desire to live differently today.

"Live as people who are free, not using your freedom as a cover-up for evil, but living as servants of God." 1 Peter 2:16

"For freedom Christ has set us free; stand firm therefore, and do not submit again to a yoke of slavery." Galatians 5:1

2. Where have you been choosing the law of the world over the law of freedom? Where have you been living for the things of the world instead of choosing life in the Spirit of God?

"There is therefore now no condemnation for those who are in Christ Jesus. For the law of the Spirit of life has set you free in Christ Jesus from the law of sin and death. For God has done what the law, weakened by the flesh, could not do." Romans 8:1-3

3. Ask the Holy Spirit to help you submit yourself fully to *"the law of the Spirit of life."* Ask him to

reveal his nearness that you might know his love today. Take time to rest in his presence and bear the fruit of communing with him.

"Now the Lord is the Spirit, and where the Spirit of the Lord is, there is freedom." 2 Corinthians 3:17

"But the fruit of the Spirit is love, joy, peace, patience, kindness, goodness, faithfulness, gentleness, self-control; against such things there is no law." Galatians 5:22-23

What would it be like to live free from condemnation as Romans 8:1 tells us? What would it be like to live free from the burden of man's opinion that we could simply enjoy how God feels about us? May the Lord help you today to experience the life that comes only by choosing freedom. May he guide you into a lifestyle of continual encounters with his love. May your days be marked by the fruit of knowing him personally. And may you exhibit to the world how wonderful it is to know and experience restored relationship with the Lord of all.

Extended Reading: Galatians 5

All He Asks of Us is Love

DAY 4

DEVOTIONAL

One of the most life-giving, transformational truths of the gospel is that of everything we have to offer God, of everything in this life we have to give, he most desires our love. To love God is all-encompassing. Colossians 3:14 says, *"And above all these put on love, which binds everything together in perfect harmony."* To love God is to pursue a life of wholehearted devotion to a

"So now faith, hope, and love abide, these three; but the greatest of these is love."

1 CORINTHIANS 13:13

King who is wholeheartedly devoted to us. To love God is to place ourselves in this never-ending, blessed cycle of giving and receiving limitless love.

The simple truth that God simply wants our love frees us from frivolous pursuits. It frees us from systems and practices that are rooted in "should" rather than true desire. God will take us however he can get us. He'll take us if all we have to give is a belief that we should serve him or be with him. But he never desires to keep us in that place. He longs to love each of us to such a level that we would live and serve him out of a place of full devotion as the natural response to his overwhelming affections for us.

1 John 4:16 says, *"So we have come to know and to believe the love that God has for us. God is love, and whoever abides in love abides in God, and God abides in him."* Allow 1 John 4:16 to create an image in your mind for a second. Picture what it would be like to truly abide in God and have him abide in you. Ask

the Holy Spirit to give you a vision of what that would be like. What would everyday life look like if you were to truly abide in God and have him abiding in you?

So great is God's love for us that he makes himself available for us to abide in him. So great are his affections for us that we could have him abiding in us. If we will pursue love above all else, we will discover a wellspring of simplicity and life rooted in wholehearted devotion to the God of love.

Cast off all other pursuits today in light of God's call to love. Cast off the striving and tireless work of doing life rooted in the "should" and let God love you to a place of love-based obedience. Find rest today in the truth that God is simply after your heart. Open up to him and receive his vast affections. 1 Corinthians 16:14 says, *"Let all that you do be done in love."* May you abide in the heart of your heavenly Father and allow him to come in and meet with you that all you do today might be done in love.

GUIDED PRAYER

1. Meditate on the call of God to love. Allow Scripture to fill you with a wholehearted desire to love God in all you do.

"You shall love the Lord your God with all your heart and with all your soul and with all your strength and with all your mind, and your neighbor as yourself." Luke 10:27

"So we have come to know and to believe the love that God has for us. God is love, and whoever abides in love abides in God, and God abides in him." 1 John 4:16

2. Ask the Holy Spirit to fill you with a fresh revelation of God's love for you. Receive the love of God and allow it to cast out all fear and reservation.

"There is no fear in love, but perfect love casts out fear. For fear has to do with punishment, and whoever fears has not been perfected in love." 1 John 4:18

3. Respond to the affections of God with your own. Tell God how you feel in his presence. Thank him for all that he's done for you. Enter into the cycle of giving and receiving affection.

"We love because he first loved us." 1 John 4:19

This cycle of giving and receiving affection is really just a picture of what it is to worship. As we allow God to love us, our natural response will be to love him in return because we are created for worship. As we receive his love we will naturally love him and others. For a long time I pictured worship as this time where I had to drum up affection for God that I honestly didn't feel. God never asks us to fake it. He never wants worship that isn't truly from our hearts. He knows we need his love to love him in return. If you find yourself emptied of affection for him and others today, take time to simply let him love you so that you can live wholeheartedly today.

Extended Reading: 1 Corinthians 13

The Joy of a Love-based Life

DAY 5

DEVOTIONAL

In God we have access to the fullness of joy. In Psalm 16:11 David says to God, *"You make known to me the path of life; in your presence there is fullness of joy; at your right hand are pleasures forevermore."* God has set out for us all a path to the fullness of joy found only in his presence, and that path is marked by love. We can have joy in and out of every season because God never stops loving us.

*"Rejoice in the Lord always;
again I will say, Rejoice."*

PHILIPPIANS 4:4

When we base our lives on the love of God rather than the thoughts, perspectives, and pursuits of the world, we position ourselves to live filled with the joy that comes solely through relationship with the Holy Spirit. Romans 14:17 says, *"For the kingdom of God is not a matter of eating and drinking but of righteousness and peace and joy in the Holy Spirit."* We have been ransomed from the ways of this world and brought into the kingdom of our heavenly Father. And in this kingdom we discover a wealth of joy found in the Spirit of God dwelling with us.

The Holy Spirit longs to make us a joyful people. He longs to lead us away from that which will steal our joy and guide us to green pastures and still waters. But a choice remains constantly before us. Will we choose the stress, burdens, and insecurities of this world or will we follow God into a more abundant life of his joy-filled presence? We have a very real enemy tempting us every day to choose a world that will never fulfill us. While we may not be his any longer, he will do whatever he can to rob us of the abundant life afforded us by the powerful sacrifice of Jesus. But 1 John 4:4 tells us, *"Little children, you are from God and have overcome them, for he who is in you is greater than he who is in the world."*

The Holy Spirit dwelling within us is perfectly capable of guiding us away from the temptations of the enemy and toward the joy that can only be found in living for God's kingdom. If we will choose today to be loved by God and love him in return, we will undoubtedly be filled with joy. Joy is a consistent symptom of seeking first the kingdom of God because his kingdom is marked by joy.

Philippians 4:4 says, *"Rejoice in the Lord always; again I will say, Rejoice."* I pray that your life will be marked by rejoicing today. I pray that you will so encounter the love of God that you are filled with joy in all you do. Choose today to base your life on the unconditional love of your heavenly Father. Choose to love him and others in all you do in response to the wealth of affections he has for you. Experience his love today and be filled with inexpressible joy.

Take time in guided prayer to encounter God's presence, commit your day to the wholehearted pursuit of love, and receive the joy available to you in God's kingdom.

GUIDED PRAYER

1. Ask God to make you aware of his nearness. Receive his presence into your heart and rest in the joy and that comes with it.

"You make known to me the path of life; in your presence there is fullness of joy; at your right hand are pleasures forevermore." Psalm 16:11

"You will seek me and find me, when you seek me with all your heart." Jeremiah 29:13

2. Commit yourself to pursuing love today in all you do. Ask the Holy Spirit to help you love God and people with your thoughts, actions, emotions, and words.

"Let all that you do be done in love." 1 Corinthians 16:14

"A new commandment I give to you, that you love one another: just as I have loved you, you also are to love one another. By this all people will know that you are my disciples, if you have love for one another." John 13:34-35

3. Receive the joy of the Holy Spirit. Ask him to bear the fruit of joy in your heart, work, and relationships. Ask him to transform you into a person marked by joy.

"For the kingdom of God is not a matter of eating and drinking but of righteousness and peace and joy in the Holy Spirit." Romans 14:17

Matthew 6:33 says, *"But seek first the kingdom of God and his righteousness, and all these things will be added to you."* This life is too short to live for anything but the kingdom of God. All other kingdoms fall away. Anything we build up that is of this world will return to dust just like us. Make the choice to live for a greater purpose than worldly acceptance and discover the wellspring of joy available to you in the kingdom of your loving heavenly Father.

Extended Reading: Matthew 6

Love-based Obedience

DEVOTIONAL

For much of my life I feared the thought of obedience, especially to the almighty, all-knowing, and all-powerful Creator of the universe. I couldn't seem to find a way to consistently choose him over myself. I couldn't seem to be able to live for his affections over those of the world. As hard as I would try in various seasons, I just couldn't be obedient.

What I didn't realize about God's command to be obedient was the process by which I could grow in obedience. God will take our obedience however he can get it because he wants us to enjoy the incredible fruits of his perfect will, but his desire is always to love us to a place that our obedience would be a natural overflow of our love for him. He longs for us to live a lifestyle of love-based obedience.

John 14:15 says very simply, *"If you love me, you will keep my commandments."* Jesus' words here are a promise. If we truly love him, we will keep his commandments. If we truly have love in our hearts, we can't help but be obedient to him. I long to grow to the place where I am so in love with Jesus that I long to choose him in every situation. I long to be a servant so in love with my King that I would die for him or anyone else he asked me to.

The love of God is so real, so powerful, and so transformational that it can mold and shape us into people who no longer live for this temporal world but seek first an everlasting, invisible kingdom. If we will simply be people who let God love us in every moment, we will naturally be people who are obedient to God's perfect will for us.

Romans 6:17-18 says, *"But thanks be to God, that you who were once slaves of sin have become obedient from the heart to the standard of teaching to which you were committed, and, having been set free from sin, have become slaves of righteousness."* Through the powerful sacrifice of Jesus, you have been transformed into a person who has gained freedom from the law of sin. You are now enslaved to a lifestyle of right living whereby you obey your King out of devotion to him.

Take time in guided prayer today to receive the transformational love of your heavenly Father. Allow his love to lay a foundation on which you pursue wholehearted obedience. May you be filled with affection for your King today as you receive the wealth of unconditional love he has for you.

GUIDED PRAYER

1. Open your heart to God to allow him to come in and love you. Ask him to guide you into a powerful encounter with his love today. Ask him to make you aware of his nearness and heart for you.

"And to know the love of Christ that surpasses knowledge, that you may be filled with all the fullness of God." Ephesians 3:19

2. Meditate on verses about obedience. Ask the Holy Spirit to transform you into a person who obeys God's commands out of love for him.

"Whoever has my commandments and keeps them, he it is who loves me. And he who loves me will be loved by my Father, and I will love him and manifest myself to him." John 14:21

"Jesus answered him, 'If anyone loves me, he will keep my word, and my Father will love him, and we will come to him and make our home with him.'" John 14:23

3. Commit yourself to obey God's commands out of trust and affection for him. Choose to serve him and those he's placed in your life. Ask him to fill you with a desire to do his will that your obedience wouldn't take debate but rather be a seamless action flowing from the love he's placed within you.

"But the word is very near you. It is in your mouth and in your heart, so that you can do it." Deuteronomy 30:14

"Therefore be imitators of God, as beloved children. And walk in love, as Christ loved us and gave himself up for us, a fragrant offering and sacrifice to God." Ephesians 5:1-2

Imagine how blessed our lives would be if we lived in total obedience to the will of God. Imagine the impact we would leave on this world. Imagine the wealth of heavenly reward we would have for all eternity. How wonderful is the heart of our heavenly Father that he would love us into a place of obedience to him, and then reward us and others for it! Our obedience is solely based on accepting his grace, and yet he loves to bless us through it. Praise be to our loving heavenly Father for the incredible life he's given us at such a great cost. May we love him in all we do.

Extended Reading: John 14

Love-based Simplicity

DAY 7

DEVOTIONAL

God's command to love affords us a life of simplicity that can only be found in his kingdom come to earth. Colossians 3:14 says, *"And above all these put on love, which binds everything together in perfect harmony."* Christianity is a simple religion. Jesus said that all of God's commandments can be summed up with one word: love. Galatians 5:14

"And above all these put on love, which binds everything together in perfect harmony."

COLOSSIANS 3:14

says, *"For the whole law is fulfilled in one word: 'You shall love your neighbor as yourself.'"* How is it then that our spirituality often feels so complex and difficult? How is that we have a hard time experiencing the simplicity our faith affords us?

Complexity in Christianity finds its root in the attempt to live for both the world and God. Jesus makes it clear in Matthew 6:24, *"No one can serve two masters, for either he will hate the one and love the other, or he will be devoted to the one and despise the other. You cannot serve God and money."* Loving God and people is simple. There is only one right choice before us in all that we do. Complexity enters into our lives as soon as we try and juggle living for the world and living for God. There is a fence between this world and God's kingdom too high to straddle. It is impossible to put one foot in God's kingdom while keeping a foot in the world.

God longs for you and me to make our first action every day to serve and love him alone. He longs to guide us into the incredible, abundant life that comes

from seeking his kingdom above all else. 1 John 2:15-17 tells us, *"Do not love the world or the things in the world. If anyone loves the world, the love of the Father is not in him. For all that is in the world—the desires of the flesh and the desires of the eyes and pride of life—is not from the Father but is from the world. And the world is passing away along with its desires, but whoever does the will of God abides forever."* You cannot have both love for the world and love for your heavenly Father. This world is at enmity with God (James 4:4). It is set against him and his ways. But you and I have been given a choice by the powerful sacrifice of Jesus. We've been given a real, available option to serve and love the eternal, Almighty God.

It's time for the bride of Christ to end its affair with the world. It's time for us to let God love us and in response live for him alone. It's time for us to *"lay aside every weight, and sin which clings so closely, and let us run with endurance the race that is set before us"* (Hebrews 12:1). Choose today the simplicity of love. Serve God alone. And discover a life far greater than anything you could experience outside of living for God above all else.

GUIDED PRAYER

1. Meditate on the impossibility of loving God and the world. Allow Scripture to fill you with a desire to seek God first today in all that you do.

"You adulterous people! Do you not know that friendship with the world is enmity with God? Therefore whoever wishes to be a friend of the world makes himself an enemy of God." James 4:4

"No one can serve two masters, for either he will hate the one and love the other, or he will be devoted to the one and despise the other. You cannot serve God and money." Matthew 6:24

2. How have you been in friendship with the world? In what ways are you trying to serve two masters?

"Do not be conformed to this world, but be transformed by the renewal of your mind, that by testing you may discern what is the will of God, what is good and acceptable and perfect." Romans 12:2

3. Confess any sin of pursuing the world to God and receive his forgiveness and love. God has total grace for us in our sin. All he wants is to guide us to a life more filled with his presence, love, and purpose. Don't wallow in your sin. Receive God's gift of forgiveness and choose to live differently.

"If we confess our sins, he is faithful and just to forgive us our sins and to cleanse us from all unrighteousness." 1 John 1:9

It's incredibly important as believers to acknowledge both our sin and the powerful transformation through God's love that's available to us. So often we allow our past sins and present failures to define us. In reality, we're given an opportunity every day to receive God's transformation and healing that we might live more like Jesus. Lamentations 3:23 tells us that his mercies are new every morning. If you will receive the mercies available to you today, you can choose to live your life differently. Have faith in the power of the Holy Spirit who dwells within you to help you. Ask him to show you the root of your sin that you might receive healing and transformation. May you discover today a wonderful life rooted in the simplicity of love.

Extended Reading: James 4

Love God

02

"God is love, and whoever abides in love abides in God, and God abides in him." 1 John 4:16

WEEKLY OVERVIEW

As we learned last week, the Christian life is meant to be marked by simplicity. Jesus summed up our purpose with two statements: love God and love people. But in our humanity we have made complex what God designed to be peaceful, purposeful, and simple. A. W. Tozer remarks in *The Pursuit of God*, "Every age has its own characteristics. Right now we are in an age of religious complexity. The simplicity which is in Christ is rarely found among us. In its stead are programs, methods, organizations and a world of nervous activities which occupy time and attention but can never satisfy the longing of the heart. The shallowness of our inner experience, the hollowness of our worship, and that servile imitation of the world which marks our promotional methods all testify that we in this day, know God only imperfectly, and the peace of God scarcely at all. If we would find God amid all the religious externals, we must first determine to find Him, and then proceed in the way of simplicity." May we discover the peace and joy that come from pursuing a simple Christianity this week.

Love God: It's All about Relationship

DAY 8

DEVOTIONAL

The world is an exhausted place. We search constantly for what should be most important or what deserves our attention from moment to moment. As the tides of societal values ebb and flow, so do our affections. We invest value and love into that which offers us nothing in return. And unfortunately the cares of this world have creeped into the people of God. Our gatherings are often marked by complexity and exhaustion. With program goals and achievements, we make complex

> *"You shall love the Lord your God with all your*
> *heart and with all your soul and with all your mind.*
> *This is the great and first commandment."*

MATTHEW 22:37-38

what God intended to be so blessedly simple. We give our attention, energy, and love to that which isn't always rooted in simply loving God.

When asked to highlight the most important commandment in all of Scripture, Jesus responded, *"You shall love the Lord your God with all your heart and with all your soul and with all your mind. This is the great and first commandment"* (Matthew 22:37-38). All of Christianity boils down to this one pursuit. And because we are to pursue loving God in all we do, all of life boils down to this single pursuit. Every single thing we do, whether it involves work, family, friends, church, entertainment, school, or solitude, is meant to be marked by the simplicity of loving God.

At the end of our days, the way we loved our heavenly Father will matter most. Our love for God matters more than any achievement, success, or program. It matters more than any possession, status, or relationship. And when we align our perspective with the first and greatest commandment, everything else comes into focus. When we pursue loving God above all else, all other pursuits fall into their proper places.

We were not created to offer our affections to anyone or anything but God first and foremost. To do otherwise is simply idolatry, and it will ruin the heavenly peace and simplicity God intends for his children. We create our own golden calves and ask them to satisfy us in ways only God can. We look to the world to offer us love it never had to begin with. But your heavenly Father is a wellspring of love and affection for you.

The commonly quoted verse John 3:16 says, *"For God so loved the world, that he gave his only Son, that whoever believes in him should not perish but have eternal life."* You will never be satisfied until you rest in the powerfully simple truth of Scripture that God has loved you and will always love you. And you will never experience the fullness of what Christ died to give you until you respond to his ceaseless love by crowning him Lord and loving him with every fiber of your being.

May you come to realize the beauty and fulfillment of a life lived in pursuit of God above all else as you spend time in prayer.

GUIDED PRAYER

1. Meditate on the first and greatest commandment. Allow Scripture to be your foundation for truth and life.

"You shall love the Lord your God with all your heart and with all your soul and with all your mind. This is the great and first commandment." Matthew 22:37-38

2. Reflect on your own life. What pursuits have become more important than loving God? What are you giving energy and affection to above relationship with your heavenly Father? What areas of your life are not being done as worship?

"Father, I desire that they also, whom you have given me, may be with me where I am, to see my glory that you have given me because you loved me before the foundation of the world. O righteous Father, even though the world does not know you, I know you, and these know that you have sent me. I made known to them your name, and I will continue to make it known, that the love with which you have loved me may be in them, and I in them." John 17:24-26

3. Confess your pursuits and receive God's loving forgiveness. Crown him as Lord of your heart and life, and ask him to help you respond to his love with your own. Ask the Spirit to help you do all that is set before you as worship to your King. Take time to give him your affections now. Worship him. Thank him. Love him. Offer him the deepest places of your heart.

"So we have come to know and to believe the love that God has for us. God is love, and whoever abides in love abides in God, and God abides in him." 1 John 4:16

You were created for worship. And until all that you do is done as worship to God, you will not experience the fullness of peace, joy, and purpose available to you through Christ. Rest, fun, work, friends, family, and church are all to be filled with the joy of loving God and being loved by him. He is the God of fun, parties, rest, and love. He has the absolute most abundant and joyful life in store for you if you will simply love him first and foremost. May you experience deeper relationship with your heavenly Father today and love him as he has loved you.

Extended Reading: Matthew 22

Love People

DAY 9

DEVOTIONAL

As we step into a deeper abundance of relationship with our heavenly Father, our hearts will naturally burn to love people as he has loved us. Loving people was never a chore for Jesus. He loved those around him with the fiery passion of his Father, and God calls you and me to do the same.

1 John 4:9-12 says, *"In this the love of God was made manifest among us, that God sent his only Son into the world, so that we might live through him. In this is love, not that we have loved God but that he loved us and*

*"Beloved, let us love one another, for love is from God,
and whoever loves has been born of God and knows God."*

sent his Son to be the propitiation for our sins. Beloved, if God so loved us, we also ought to love one another. No one has ever seen God; if we love one another, God abides in us and his love is perfected in us." God's love, perfected in you, will be demonstrated in the way you love others. Allow that fact to rest in your heart for a minute. Allow Scripture to establish in you the core value of selfless love.

I used to think that the highest form of Christian spirituality would be surrendering all forms of pleasure and human contact in order to devote my entire life to relationship with God. But Scripture is clear that God desires to produce in us a passionate pursuit and love for everyone around us. We demonstrate the depth of our love for him through the depth of our love for others. Christianity is not a religion of cliques, comfort zones, or isolation. Rather, it is a personal relationship with a God who loves people and longs to fill us with his love for others.

Our heavenly Father knows that we are incapable of consistently and selflessly loving others in our own strength. He knows that apart from him we are selfish,

prideful, fearful, and inconsistent. But our God is fully capable of remarkable transformation if we will open the doors of our hearts to his love and allow him to change us for the better. If we will allow him to satisfy us and heal our wounds, we will receive a flood of genuine love for others that casts out all fear, selfishness, and pride in light of God's glorious grace.

Jesus said in John 15:12-14, *"This is my commandment, that you love one another as I have loved you. Greater love has no one than this, that someone lay down his life for his friends. You are my friends if you do what I command you."* What is holding you back from loving others selflessly? Where do you need a fresh filling of God's love to heal your wounds and satisfy your heart? What fear or source of pride is keeping you from receiving God's passionate heart for others around you?

Spend time in prayer allowing Scripture to influence and reprioritize what you view as most important. Allow God to flood the dry and wounded places of your heart. And allow the Holy Spirit to fill you with his heart for those around you who desperately need someone to reveal God's love to them.

GUIDED PRAYER

1. Meditate on Jesus' commandment to love others in response to his love. Allow Scripture to lay the foundation for how you will decide to live your life.

"In this the love of God was made manifest among us, that God sent his only Son into the world, so that we might live through him. In this is love, not that we have loved God but that he loved us and sent his Son to be the propitiation for our sins. Beloved, if God so loved us, we also ought to love one another. No one has ever seen God; if we love one another, God abides in us and his love is perfected in us." 1 John 4:9-12

"By this all people will know that you are my disciples, if you have love for one another." John 13:35

"Owe no one anything, except to love each other, for the one who loves another has fulfilled the law. For the commandments, 'You shall not commit adultery, You shall not murder, You shall not steal, You shall not covet,' and any other commandment, are summed up in this word: 'You shall love your neighbor as yourself.' Love does no wrong to a neighbor; therefore love is the fulfilling of the law." Romans 13:8-10

2. Spend time receiving God's love. Where do you need his love in order to love others well? What wound is causing you to live fearfully, selfishly, or pridefully? What area of your life needs to be healed or satisfied? Ask God to pinpoint that place.

"So that Christ may dwell in your hearts through faith—that you, being rooted and grounded in love, may have strength to comprehend with all the saints what is the breadth and length and height and depth, and to know the love of Christ that surpasses knowledge, that you may be filled with all the fullness of God." Ephesians 3:17-19

3. Ask the Holy Spirit to fill you with God's heart for others. Allow him to show you how he feels about people at your work, school, church, or neighborhood. Ask him to reveal specific people he desires you to love well today. Ask him for specific ways he would have you love them.

"This is my commandment, that you love one another as I have loved you. Greater love has no one than this, that someone lay down his life for his friends. You are my friends if you do what I command you." John 15:12-14

"Let love be genuine. Abhor what is evil; hold fast to what is good. Love one another with brotherly affection. Outdo one another in showing honor." Romans 12:9-10

The ability to genuinely love others is a sign of the new nature placed within you at salvation. Genuine love is not of this world, but of the kingdom of God. When you love selflessly you bring the kingdom of heaven to earth. The world has no rebuttal for love. It has no grid for acts of selfless generosity. Love tears down walls that have been built up between man and God. It pierces through hard exteriors and reaches the core of man's heart. May you reveal the great love of your heavenly Father today through acts of genuine, selfless love.

Extended Reading: John 15

A Life of Sacrifice

DAY 10

DEVOTIONAL

Living for our own gain adds stress, pressure, and chaos to life, successfully robbing us of all the transcendent peace available through sacrificial living. We were never created to be our own provider or sustainer. We were never meant to develop our own source of joy and purpose. The only place we will find lasting peace is in complete surrender to God's intention for us: a life of total sacrifice.

Jesus was our perfect model. He did everything according to the perfect and pleasing will of the Father. And Jesus said in Luke 9:23-25, *"If anyone would come after me, let him deny himself and take up his cross daily and follow me. For whoever would save his life will lose it, but whoever loses his life for my sake will save it. For what does it profit a man if he gains the whole world and loses or forfeits himself?"* Jesus makes it clear that sacrifice is the gateway to finding the life God intends for us. It's the pathway that leads to the perfect will of our heavenly Father.

If you're like me, living life sacrificially initially sounds terrible and unattainable. It feels impossible based on past experiences and present selfish desires. But, we need to take time to know the God to whom we are

> *"If anyone would come after me, let him deny himself and take up his cross daily and follow me."*
>
> **LUKE 9:23**

sacrificing our lives. We need to renew our mind to the perfect love of Jesus who would lay down his own life for us before ever asking us to follow in his footsteps. The life God intends for you is better than anything you could discover on your own. If he's asking you to live sacrificially it must be wholly and perfectly for your benefit.

We are not sacrificing our own wills, plans, and dreams to a God who has less satisfying plans for our lives. We are not surrendering a happier, better life for something less, boring, or meaningless. Jesus said in John 10:10, *"I came that they may have life and have it abundantly."*

God has plans greater than we could ever ask or imagine in store for us if we will lay down our dreams to make space for his. He has inexpressible joy for us if we will exchange what has made us temporarily happy for his dreams and visions that are full of purpose, meaning, and adventure.

Jesus willingly laid down his life and received everything he had dreamed of: restored relationship with you. What's waiting for you on the other side of sacrifice today? Find out as you engage in the act of surrender during guided prayer.

GUIDED PRAYER

1. Meditate on Jesus' command for you to live your life sacrificially. Reflect on God's desire to lead you to abundant life through surrender and sacrifice.

"If anyone would come after me, let him deny himself and take up his cross daily and follow me. For whoever would save his life will lose it, but whoever loses his life for my sake will save it. For what does it profit a man if he gains the whole world and loses or forfeits himself?" Luke 9:23-25

"I came that they may have life and have it abundantly." John 10:10

2. What do you need to surrender to the Father? What dream, idea, person, or possession is robbing you of the abundant life God intends for you. Where do you need to live sacrificially to experience more of Jesus? Surrender whatever stands in the way of you and the abundant life God has for you.

"Do not love the world or the things in the world. If anyone loves the world, the love of the Father is not in him." 1 John 2:15

3. Choose to live sacrificially today. Ask the Holy Spirit to make the will of the Father known to you as he did for Jesus, and commit to following whatever he is asking you to do.

"Have this mind among yourselves, which is yours in Christ Jesus, who, though he was in the form of God, did not count equality with God a thing to be grasped, but emptied himself, by taking the form of a servant, being born in the likeness of men. And being found in human form, he humbled himself by becoming obedient to the point of death, even death on a cross." Philippians 2:5-8

Taking up your cross isn't a weight designed to burden and constrain you, but an opportunity to live in the presence, peace, and purpose of God. There is freedom in store for you through sacrifice. There is purpose and joy in laying down your life for God and others. If you will receive the perspective and courage to pursue God's will for your life, you will discover more peace, consistency, passion, and direction than you ever thought possible.

Extended Reading: Philippians 2

Rest in God

DAY 11

DEVOTIONAL

One of the simple, core values of restored relationship with our heavenly Father is rest. From the beginning God exemplified its importance. Genesis 2:3 says, *"God blessed the seventh day and made it holy, because on it God rested from all his work that he had done in creation."* And Hebrews 4:9-13 says,

"Come to me, all who labor and are heavy laden, and I will give you rest. Take my yoke upon you, and learn from me, for I am gentle and lowly in heart, and you will find rest for your souls. For my yoke is easy, and my burden is light."

MATTHEW 11:28-30

So then, there remains a Sabbath rest for the people of God, for whoever has entered God's rest has also rested from his works as God did from his. Let us therefore strive to enter that rest, so that no one may fall by the same sort of disobedience. For the word of God is living and active, sharper than any two-edged sword, piercing to the division of soul and of spirit, of joints and of marrow, and discerning the thoughts and intentions of the heart. And no creature is hidden from his sight, but all are naked and exposed to the eyes of him to whom we must give account.

I fear that we as children of God have allowed the busyness and stress of the world to influence us in greater ways than the *"living and active"* word of our heavenly Father. We are designed for rest. We are designed to have a full day and various times throughout each day set aside to simply enjoy God and the blessed life he has given us. When we value success and busyness over relationship with God and obedience to his commands, our priorities begin to fall out of place. When we choose busyness over rest, we place more value on whatever we are working toward than on our restored relationship with God and the abundant life he died to give us.

We are created to work. Prior to sin entering the story of humanity, Adam and Eve labored for God. Work is not a symptom of the fall but rather an incredible joy and privilege given to us by the hand of our Father. But our society promotes a lie that resting is directly related to laziness or selfishness and working is always good. Too much work takes us outside of the grace and provision of God for our work and forces us to labor in our own strength. God has perfect plans and grace for everything he has laid before you, but it is often in rest that you will be refueled and made ready to receive that grace to accomplish your tasks. It's in rest that our souls are restored, replenished, and filled. And it's in rest that we are able to take time to be thankful and celebrate what God has helped us accomplish, rather than always bearing the burden of the never-ending list of tasks before us.

May we be children who choose to live by the word and systems of God rather than the values and structures of the world. May we be children who live with the simple, core value of rest as we follow the model of our heavenly Father.

59

GUIDED PRAYER

1. Meditate on God's desire to bring you rest.
Allow Scripture to renew your mind and transform the way you make decisions and live.

"Six days you shall work, but on the seventh day you shall rest. In plowing time and in harvest you shall rest." Exodus 34:21

"So then, there remains a Sabbath rest for the people of God, for whoever has entered God's rest has also rested from his works as God did from his. Let us therefore strive to enter that rest, so that no one may fall by the same sort of disobedience. For the word of God is living and active, sharper than any two-edged sword, piercing to the division of soul and of spirit, of joints and of marrow, and discerning the thoughts and intentions of the heart. And no creature is hidden from his sight, but all are naked and exposed to the eyes of him to whom we must give account." Hebrews 4:9-13

2. Where have you forgone rest for busyness and work? In what ways have you allowed society to influence you more than God's word?

3. Confess to God any ways in which you have forsaken rest and receive his forgiveness. Ask God to fill you with a fresh vision for his purposes behind rest. Ask him to guide you into a lifestyle of taking a Sabbath. Rest in him right now, and allow him to replenish and rejuvenate you with his presence.

"Come to me, all who labor and are heavy laden, and I will give you rest. Take my yoke upon you, and learn from me, for I am gentle and lowly in heart, and you will find rest for your souls. For my yoke is easy, and my burden is light." Matthew 11:28-30

A large part of being led by the Spirit is following where God's grace takes you. God has grace and provision for every task he has laid before you. He will help you accomplish everything you need to do in a timely and productive fashion. If you don't feel grace for whatever task is before you, take time to ask the Spirit what he would have you do. Sometimes he will replenish you on the spot so you can keep working. Other times he'll have something else for you to do instead. But often he will guide you into a few moments of rest and finding satisfaction in him so that you can work with proper perspective and his strength rather than just your own. May you work and rest in the grace and glory of your heavenly Father today.

Extended Reading: Hebrews 4

61

The Discipline of Simplicity

DAY 12

DEVOTIONAL

Often, we are kept from living lives marked by the joy and peace of our heavenly Father because of our continual pursuit for more. Humanity's first sin was pursuing more than God intended for us, and the enemy continues to entice us with that temptation today. A core value of the world is more: more money, more fame, more friends, more success, more happiness,

"For our boast is this, the testimony of our conscience, that we behaved in the world with simplicity and godly sincerity, not by earthly wisdom but by the grace of God, and supremely so toward you."

2 CORINTHIANS 1:12

more possessions, more of anything, because we feel dissatisfied with our lives. We are constantly grabbing for that which will never fully satisfy in the present or lead us to a lifestyle of continual satisfaction.

Paul writes in 2 Corinthians 1:12, *"For our boast is this, the testimony of our conscience, that we behaved in the world with simplicity and godly sincerity, not by earthly wisdom but by the grace of God, and supremely so toward you."* Simplicity is a God-given discipline that prunes the dead branches of waste that effactually deplete us of the energy, time, and provision with which God has blessed us. When we make the decision to stop pursuing more, we step in line with the Spirit and place our trust and faith in God rather than our own understanding.

You see, at the core of a continual pursuit for more is a lack of faith in God's goodness. If we truly believed God provides all we need, we would never step outside his provision and strive for more. Adam and Eve questioned God's goodness and thereby brought the destructive nature of sin into humanity. They decided for themselves what was enough rather than trusting God to know what was best for them.

Our own forbidden fruit takes on all sorts of forms. We work our fingers to the bone for a taste of greater success all the while forgetting who it is we are to work for in the first place. We take God-given financial provision and waste it on worldly pleasures rather than investing it into that which will actually satisfy us. We take what we receive from God and use it to finance self-indulgence rather than sharing it with those whom God wanted to use us to bless from the beginning. And we take the valuable resource of time and waste it on pursuits that were never God's intention to begin with.

We desperately need transformation and training in the discipline of simplicity. In order to experience joy and peace that transcends circumstances and position ourselves through faithfulness to receive more of what God longs to give, we must offer our time, energy, and money to God and follow the guidance of his Spirit and word.

Matthew 6:21 says, *"For where your treasure is, there your heart will be also."* Take time in guided prayer placing all your treasure in the only place that can offer you eternal investment: with your heavenly Father.

63

GUIDED PRAYER

1. Meditate on the importance of simplicity and the destructive pursuit of more.

"No servant can serve two masters, for either he will hate the one and love the other, or he will be devoted to the one and despise the other. You cannot serve God and money." Luke 16:13

"Look carefully then how you walk, not as unwise but as wise, making the best use of the time, because the days are evil. Therefore do not be foolish, but understand what the will of the Lord is." Ephesians 5:15-17

2. Reflect on areas of your life that are not marked by simplicity. Ask the Spirit to convict you of anything you need to get rid of. It's incredibly important to note the difference between guilt and conviction. Conviction from the Spirit is always done in love and will always bring you inner peace and joy as you follow through in obedience.

"But the fruit of the Spirit is love, joy, peace, patience, kindness, goodness, faithfulness, gentleness, self-control; against such things there is no law." Galatians 5:22-23

3. Commit to ending the pursuit of more by trusting in the provision and goodness of your heavenly Father. Place your trust in him alone, and ask him to guide you into a lifestyle of simplicity.

"Therefore do not be anxious, saying, 'What shall we eat?' or 'What shall we drink?' or 'What shall we wear?' For

the Gentiles seek after all these things, and your heavenly Father knows that you need them all. But seek first the kingdom of God and his righteousness, and all these things will be added to you." Matthew 6:31-33

"For our boast is this, the testimony of our conscience, that we behaved in the world with simplicity and godly sincerity, not by earthly wisdom but by the grace of God, and supremely so toward you." 2 Corinthians 1:12

God has different plans for each of his children. He intends for some to live in poverty with absolutely no possessions, while others he wants to bless in abundance that they may have the privilege of co-laboring with him in blessing others. Scripture is clear that our God gives good and perfect gifts. He loves to bless his children. To live simply, we just need to live in continual relationship with the Holy Spirit and allow him to show us what gifts are from him and whether they are for our benefit or pleasure or to give away to others. May you find greater depths of peace as you grow in trusting God and following the perfect and abundant leadership of the Holy Spirit.

Extended Reading: 2 Corinthians 1

The Simple Truth of Freedom from Sin

DAY 13

DEVOTIONAL

2 Corinthians 3:18 says, *"Now the Lord is the Spirit, and where the Spirit of the Lord is, there is freedom."* Freedom from sin is not something we pay for with our own blood, sweat, and tears. It is not bought by any measure of human strength or will, but by the precious and powerful blood of Jesus Christ. Scripture tells clearly of the pervasive and

"Now the Lord is the Spirit,
and where the Spirit of the Lord
is, there is freedom."

2 CORINTHIANS 3:17

liberating effects of Jesus' death for all those who come to believe in him and claim him as Lord. May we be children freed from the bonds of slavery Christ died to set us free from.

Romans 8:1-4 says,

There is therefore now no condemnation for those who are in Christ Jesus. For the law of the Spirit of life has set you free in Christ Jesus from the law of sin and death. For God has done what the law, weakened by the flesh, could not do. By sending his own Son in the likeness of sinful flesh and for sin, he condemned sin in the flesh, in order that the righteous requirement of the law might be fulfilled in us, who walk not according to the flesh but according to the Spirit.

With the filling of the Spirit came a new law, a new covenant by which the chains of sin are broken. We are no longer condemned to live under the tyranny of sin, but rather freed to live under the new law of the Spirit. And *"where the Spirit of the Lord is, there is freedom."*

The simple truth of Scripture in regards to sin is that freedom is ours through Christ Jesus. To experience true freedom from sin is to simply live in light of the powerful infilling of the Holy Spirit and the living and active word of God's truth about you. Romans 6:6, 18 and 22 say, *"We know that our old self was crucified with him in order that the body of sin might be brought to nothing, so that we would no longer be enslaved to sin . . . . And, having been set free from sin, have become slaves of righteousness . . . . Now that you have been set free from sin and have become slaves of God, the fruit you get leads to sanctification and its end, eternal life."*

You are a slave of this world no longer. Your past does not define you. The future before you is one of peace, joy, and freedom in the Spirit. God has incredible plans in store for you that far surpass simply overcoming sin. Jesus died to give you abundant life here in which freedom and love are your portion, not habitual sin and destruction.

Renew your mind to the law of the Spirit to which you now belong as you spend time in guided prayer.

GUIDED PRAYER

1. Meditate on the freedom available to you through the death of Christ and infilling of the Holy Spirit. Allow Scripture to renew your mind and change your perspective on sin and freedom.

"We know that our old self was crucified with him in order that the body of sin might be brought to nothing, so that we would no longer be enslaved to sin." Romans 6:6

"Now the Lord is the Spirit, and where the Spirit of the Lord is, there is freedom." 2 Corinthians 3:17

"There is therefore now no condemnation for those who are in Christ Jesus. For the law of the Spirit of life has set you free in Christ Jesus from the law of sin and death. For God has done what the law, weakened by the flesh, could not do. By sending his own Son in the likeness of sinful flesh and for sin, he condemned sin in the flesh, in order that the righteous requirement of the law might be fulfilled in us, who walk not according to the flesh but according to the Spirit." Romans 8:1-4

2. What sin seems to continually entangle you? What victory do you feel the enemy has over you?

3. Ask the Holy Spirit to fill you with his perspective in regards to your sin. Ask him to show you the path to freedom. View your sin through the lens of Scripture and put it in its proper place.

"And, having been set free from sin, have become slaves of righteousness." Romans 6:18

"But now that you have been set free from sin and have become slaves of God, the fruit you get leads to sanctification and its end, eternal life." Romans 6:22

"In the same way we also, when we were children, were enslaved to the elementary principles of the world. But when the fullness of time had come, God sent forth his Son, born of woman, born under the law, to redeem those who were under the law, so that we might receive adoption as sons. And because you are sons, God has sent the Spirit of his Son into our hearts, crying, 'Abba! Father!' So you are no longer a slave, but a son, and if a son, then an heir through God." Galatians 4:3-7

James 5:16 says, *"Therefore, confess your sins to one another and pray for one another, that you may be healed. The prayer of a righteous person has great power as it is working."* The act of confessing our sin to one another is powerful in experiencing the freedom available to us. Everything the devil does is in the shadows and is marked by deception. When we confess our sin, we bring it into the light, expose the lies, and are able to better see the destructive plans of the enemy. It's in the light that we experience the freedom available to us. May you be filled with courage to expose your sin and walk in the freedom of righteousness today.

Extended Reading: Romans 8

The Simplicity of Grace

DAY 14

DEVOTIONAL

Grace is a glorious commodity of heaven that can only be received and experienced in surrender to the will and love of our heavenly Father. Our world is unable to offer grace because it is in a constant state of need, and grace can only be offered from a place of true wholeness and love. In utter completeness, our God is able to offer us grace

*"But by the grace of God I am what I am, and
his grace toward me was not in vain. On the contrary,
I worked harder than any of them, though it was not
I, but the grace of God that is with me."*

1 CORINTHIANS 15:10

because he needs nothing from us in return. He requires nothing of us, so he offers us everything apart from any ability or inherent value we possess.

Grace comprises the core of the Christian foundation. It's God's grace that drove him to send his Son as payment for our sins. It's through grace that we enter into the fullness of restored relationship with our good Father. It's through grace that we receive forgiveness for our sins. And it's in the simplicity of grace that we are transformed into the very image of our Savior.

I find myself continually missing out on all that God's grace offers me. I retreat into a lifestyle of works where I try to earn what God has already given me. I work for the love of my heavenly Father and others, vying for affection rather than receiving the ceaseless love of God for me. I strive and work for holiness and righteousness instead of simply aligning myself with the new nature of freedom God has offered me in grace.

1 Corinthians 15:10 says, *"By the grace of God I am what I am, and his grace toward me was not in vain."* Can you say today that you are what you are by the grace of God? Is your life marked by and founded on God's limitless supply of grace? Are your emotions, perspectives, pursuits, and relationships founded on the notion that God loves you simply because he loves you? Have you found total security and rest in the loving embrace of a God who longs to fill you, sustain you, bless you, provide for you, and love you simply because it's his desire?

Allow God to fill you with a fresh revelation of his grace today. Come before him with an open heart, and allow the truth of his unceasing and grace-filled love wash through you. Allow him to cast out any fear, toil, or burden that is keeping you from the abundant life available to you. Spend time in guided prayer being transformed by the simplicity of grace.

GUIDED PRAYER

1. Meditate on the principles of grace. How does it work? Where does it come from? How can you experience it? Allow God's word to lay a foundation of grace by which you live.

"But by the grace of God I am what I am, and his grace toward me was not in vain. On the contrary, I worked harder than any of them, though it was not I, but the grace of God that is with me." 1 Corinthians 15:10

"For through the law I died to the law, so that I might live to God. I have been crucified with Christ. It is no longer I who live, but Christ who lives in me. And the life I now live in the flesh I live by faith in the Son of God, who loved me and gave himself for me. I do not nullify the grace of God, for if righteousness were through the law, then Christ died for no purpose." Galatians 2:19-21

2. In what ways are you living a works-based life? Where do you need a fresh vision for living by grace?

3. Ask the Holy Spirit to give you a fresh vision for how deeply God's grace goes in any and every circumstance you face. Ask him to fill you with a fresh revelation of how deeply he loves you regardless of what you do. Allow him to lead you into a lifestyle of living by grace in every pursuit, relationship, thought, and perspective.

Living in response to God's love rather than working to earn it changes everything. It eliminates the pressures of this world that are founded upon personal success in every area of life. It frees us to live joyfully and satisfied rather than incomplete and in a constant state of want. May you make time throughout your day today to receive a fresh revelation of grace. May you discover through grace the life Jesus died to freely give. May you discover how wonderful it is to be loved by a God who requires nothing of you before he gives you everything.

Extended Reading: John 1

Love people

03

WEEK

"*Beloved, let us love one another, for love is from God, and whoever loves has been born of God and knows God.*" 1 John 4:7

WEEKLY OVERVIEW

Loving others is one of the most important and difficult commands Jesus gave us. We are a messy, broken, needy, and sinful people. We constantly deal with our own wounds and those of others. Because there is no perfect person, the foundation for loving others must be based outside of the merit or worth of others. The foundation for love must come from the God who is love. As believers we must be constantly tapped into the love and grace of our heavenly Father so that we can love others selflessly and powerfully. May you receive the love of your Father and be empowered to love others this week as we look to grow in our obedience of Jesus' command to love people.

Living without Offense

DAY 15

DEVOTIONAL

Taking offense allows others to dictate your emotions and thereby your quality of life. When we allow the expressions of brokenness in others to affect us, we take our minds off of the ways of heaven and place them on the ways of the world. If we are to effectively live in obedience to the second greatest commandment of loving others, we must allow God to transform us into those who live without offense.

When someone wrongs me, I instantly feel a need for justice and fairness rise within me. I feel as if I inherently have the right to be angry or even to exact revenge for the wrong they committed. Offense stirs up feelings of insecurity, pride, anger, and frustration that I will do just about anything to rid myself of. But when I look at Scripture, I see Jesus modeling the exact opposite reaction to offense.

Matthew 27 is filled with wrongs done to Jesus. As seen in his betrayal, the freeing of the murderer Barabbas, the floggings, a crown of thorns, carrying of the cross, the mocking by the soldiers and thief, and his eventual death, Jesus had more right to take offense and exact revenge than any human in all of history. But Jesus saw past all the offense to the heart of those who wronged him. He saw past the

*"Good sense makes one slow to anger,
and it is his glory to overlook an offense."*

PROVERBS 19:11

hard, aggressive, and angry exteriors to the wounded places of the soul and found within him the strength, love, and courage to pray, *"Father, forgive them, for they know not what they do"* (Luke 23:34). In the face of the worst offenses and injustices, Jesus chose to offer grace, mercy, forgiveness, and compassion.

Jesus lived his life free from offense and therefore was freed to love others. His ability to look past expressions of brokenness to the hurts beneath the surface empowered him to live with joy, passion, love, and purpose. Leviticus 19:18 says, *"You shall not take vengeance or bear a grudge against the sons of your own people, but you shall love your neighbor as yourself: I am the Lord."* If we are to fulfill the command of Scripture, we must look to Jesus as our model and live without offense. We must choose grace over revenge and compassion over worldly justice.

You have the ability to choose how you will respond to others. Your emotions and actions do not have to be dictated by the sinful acts of others. Choose to pursue love and humility over vengeance and anger. Allow the Lord to highlight and heal any wounds and insecurities that cause you to respond poorly to offense as you enter into guided prayer.

GUIDED PRAYER

1. Meditate on Scripture's command to live without offense. Reflect on Jesus' response to offense and elevate him as your model for living.

"Good sense makes one slow to anger, and it is his glory to overlook an offense." Proverbs 19:11

"When he was reviled, he did not revile in return; when he suffered, he did not threaten, but continued entrusting himself to him who judges justly." 1 Peter 2:23

"Do nothing from selfish ambition or conceit, but in humility count others more significant than yourselves. Let each of you look not only to his own interests, but also to the interests of others. Have this mind among yourselves, which is yours in Christ Jesus, who, though he was in the form of God, did not count equality with God a thing to be grasped, but emptied himself, by taking the form of a servant, being born in the likeness of men. And being found in human form, he humbled himself by becoming obedient to the point of death, even death on a cross." Philippians 2:3-8

2. What insecurities or wounds cause you to respond to offense in ways other than those of Jesus? What's at the core of your offense? What's keeping you from fully loving others?

"Do not take to heart all the things that people say, lest you hear your servant cursing you. Your heart knows

that many times you yourself have cursed others." Ecclesiastes 7:21-22

3. Ask the Holy Spirit to help you look past acts of brokenness to the heart of those who offend you. Ask him to heal your own brokenness and transform you into a person who loves others well.

"Be kind to one another, tenderhearted, forgiving one another, as God in Christ forgave you." Ephesians 4:32

"So then let us pursue what makes for peace and for mutual upbuilding." Romans 14:19

"With all humility and gentleness, with patience, bearing with one another in love, eager to maintain the unity of the Spirit in the bond of peace." Ephesians 4:2-3

What would your life be like if you were free from offense? How much more consistently would you experience peace and joy? If God commands you to choose humility and compassion over offense, it must be a far better way to live. Vengeance, anger, and frustration will only rob you of the abundant life God intends for you, whereas humility and compassion will fill you with the very power and grace of God himself. May you be a child with the heart of the Father and love others with his love today.

Extended Reading: Matthew 27

Seeing Past the Brokenness

DAY 16

DEVOTIONAL

Without perspective given by the Spirit, our love will only reach as far as the human eye can see. Brokenness comes in all forms and fashions. Without Jesus, the man or woman covered in dirt and filth standing on the street corner begging for help is just as broken as the millionaire lying and cheating his way into fleeting fame and fortune. It's just that our brokenness takes on varying forms depending on what temptations and trials get the better of us.

> *"The Lord is near to the brokenhearted*
> *and saves the crushed in spirit."*
>
> **PSALM 34:18**

Jesus saw past the brokenness to the hearts of those around him. He chose to love and minister to the core of the person rather than being intimidated by the symptoms of sin in those around him. He saw into the heart of the woman at the well in John 4 and ministered to her brokenness caused by failed marriages and sexual sin. We see him speak to the core of the wealthy tax collector, Zacchaeus, in Luke 19 and love him by spending time with him when no one else would.

If we are ever going to love others well, we have to devote ourselves to loving people at a heart level. We have to care for and speak to the core of their wounds rather than dismissing them for their external problems. Romans 15:1-5 says:

We who are strong have an obligation to bear with the failings of the weak, and not to please ourselves. Let each of us please his neighbor for his good, to build him up. For Christ did not please himself, but as it is written, 'The reproaches of those who reproached you fell on me.'

For whatever was written in former days was written for our instruction, that through endurance and through the encouragement of the Scriptures we might have hope. May the God of endurance and encouragement grant you to live in such harmony with one another, in accord with Christ Jesus.

We must follow the example of Jesus and love those no one else will. We must take in the outcasts, orphaned, widowed, poor, prideful, arrogant, and selfish. We must have our Father's heart for the enemies, strangers, socially unacceptable, and downcast. If we don't love them, who will? If we don't speak and provide love for the deep wounds that cause their brokenness, who will? If we don't reveal the heart of our Father, who will?

Psalm 34:18 says, *"The Lord is near to the brokenhearted and saves the crushed in spirit."* May you discover the unconditional love your heavenly Father has toward those broken and crushed today as you enter into guided prayer.

85

GUIDED PRAYER

1. Meditate on the importance of seeing past brokenness to the heart of those around you. Allow Scripture to fill you with desire and purpose to love people well today.

"So then let us pursue what makes for peace and for mutual upbuilding." Romans 14:19

"And let us consider how to stir up one another to love and good works, not neglecting to meet together, as is the habit of some, but encouraging one another, and all the more as you see the Day drawing near." Hebrews 10:24-25

2. Whose brokenness has kept you from loving them well? What person would God fill you with the ability to minister to today that desperately needs a touch from God?

3. Ask the Lord for his heart for that person. Ask God to give you an understanding of what wound he wants to minister to. Ask him to give you a creative insight on how to love them well today.

"The Lord is near to the brokenhearted and saves the crushed in spirit." Psalm 34:18

Often, loving someone well can be as simple as going out of your way to say hello, ask a loving question, or make an uplifting comment. Many people just need to know that someone cares about them and notices them at the heart level. May the Lord use you in mighty ways to draw others to himself today.

Extended Reading: John 4

Jesus is
the Model

DAY 17

DEVOTIONAL

Everything Jesus did was done out of his perfect love for the Father and us. Every word, healing, prayer, and action was done out of unconditional devotion. Ephesians 5:1-2 says, *"Therefore be imitators of God, as beloved children. And walk in love, as Christ loved us and gave himself up for us, a fragrant offering and sacrifice to God."* Scripture commands us to love others the way Christ did. Jesus is our model for living. And God never commands us without perfectly equipping us. If we are to *"walk in love, as Christ loved us,"* we must believe God will fill us up with the ability to love as Jesus loved.

*"By this we know love, that he laid
down his life for us, and we ought to lay
down our lives for the brothers."*

1 JOHN 3:16

The concept of living like Jesus always seemed unreachable. It often reminded me of motivational posters that read, "Reach for the moon—even if you miss you'll land among the stars." But God's word is not an unachievable suggestion. His word is perfect and true. And Scripture says in Romans 8:29, *"For those whom he foreknew he also predestined to be conformed to the image of his Son, in order that he might be the firstborn among many brothers."* God's plan is to conform us into perfect reflections of Jesus' love. His plan is to fashion us into disciples who live, work, and love as he did.

We can live our lives in obedience to God's command to love others for one reason alone: our heavenly Father is near, alive, and active in us. The same God who empowered Paul, Peter, John, Stephen, David, Daniel, and Esther lives in us today. Romans 8:11 says, *"If the Spirit of him who raised Jesus from the dead dwells in you, he who raised Christ Jesus from the dead will also give life to your mortal bodies through his Spirit who dwells in you."* And the Bible says that the fruit of the Spirit who dwells within us as believers is love. We can love like Jesus because his Spirit longs to produce the fruit of love deep within us. He longs to love people through us. He has a perfect plan to use you to reveal to a broken and searching world the unfathomable riches of Jesus' love.

If we are to look to Jesus as our model, we must first believe that God can and will help us. We must believe that the Spirit is perfectly capable of taking what was dust and fashioning it into the likeness of the Son. Secondly, we must spend time allowing the Spirit to move in and through us. We must make space in our lives to be loved by God so that we can be used by him to love others. I can offer nothing of value that I haven't first received from my heavenly Father. I can do nothing great unless God has done something great in me. 1 John 2:6 says, *"Whoever says he abides in him ought to walk in the same way in which he walked."* We have to be children who abide in Jesus so that we can walk in his ways.

God longs to love you and help you love others today. He longs to meet you and heal the wounds and insecurities that have kept you from loving others well. He longs to empower and transform you to live like Jesus. Run to him with open arms, and allow him to do a mighty work in you as you enter into guided prayer.

GUIDED PRAYER

1. Meditate on God's desire for you to love like Jesus. Remember that God doesn't command you to do something you are incapable of doing. Allow Scripture to fill you with desire and faith for what God has for you.

"Therefore be imitators of God, as beloved children. And walk in love, as Christ loved us and gave himself up for us, a fragrant offering and sacrifice to God." Ephesians 5:1–2

"For to this you have been called, because Christ also suffered for you, leaving you an example, so that you might follow in his steps." 1 Peter 2:21

"For those whom he foreknew he also predestined to be conformed to the image of his Son, in order that he might be the firstborn among many brothers." Romans 8:29

2. Where do you need God to do a mighty work in you today? Ask the Spirit to reveal what areas he wants to heal today. Ask him to guide you to a wound or insecurity he longs to speak to and love.

3. Receive the love of your heavenly Father. Allow him to heal and empower you to love others. Ask him to transform you into the image of Jesus and fill you with his heart for others around you.

"But I say to you who hear, Love your enemies, do good to those who hate you." Luke 6:27

"Above all, keep loving one another earnestly, since love covers a multitude of sins." 1 Peter 4:8

"You have heard that it was said, 'You shall love your neighbor and hate your enemy.' But I say to you, Love your enemies and pray for those who persecute you, so that you may be sons of your Father who is in heaven. For he makes his sun rise on the evil and on the good, and sends rain on

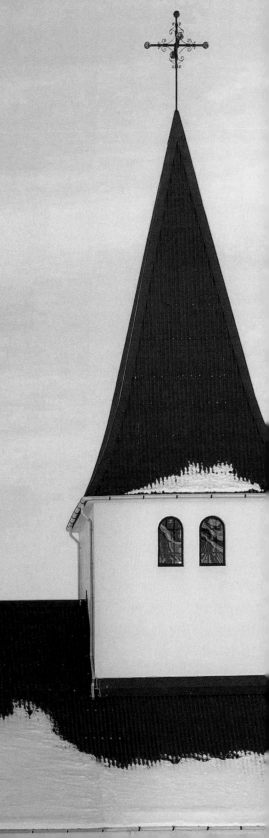

the just and on the unjust. For if you love those who love you, what reward do you have? Do not even the tax collectors do the same? And if you greet only your brothers, what more are you doing than others? Do not even the Gentiles do the same?" Matthew 5:43-47

It is impossible to be consistently loved by God and not love others. His love has this incredible ability to heal us and empower us at the same time. His heart is always to love us while helping us to love others. As you grow in your relationship with your heavenly Father, allow him to use you in increasingly powerful ways. Allow him to make you selfless and servant-hearted. Allow his love to make you more like Jesus. May you discover the joy and peace that comes from wholeheartedly loving others today.

Extended Reading: 1 John 3

Loving Family

DAY 18

DEVOTIONAL

One of the most direct examples of the kingdom of God on the earth is the family unit. God longs to use the love between family members to tell the world of his love as the Creator and Father of all. As believers, we must choose to continually love, forgive, help, and pursue strong relationships with those God has given us as our family.

*"Honor your father and your mother, that your days may
be long in the land that the Lord your God is giving you."*

EXODUS 20:12

You are not a member of your family by mistake. Psalm 139:13 says, *"For you formed my inward parts; you knitted me together in my mother's womb."* God formed you perfectly for your family. He had plans for you and your family before the formation of the heavens and the earth. And he has placed your family on the earth intentionally and purposefully. He has incredible plans for a family that will pursue love for each other and walk in his eternal purposes.

Your heavenly Father knows the follies of your family. He knows their weaknesses, trials, and temptations. But he also longs to empower you with grace to love them. He longs to use you to restore your family to him so that you might experience the wonders of God-filled family relationships.

Scripture is filled with commandments about the family unit. Exodus 20:12 says, *"Honor your father and your mother, that your days may be long in the land that the Lord your God is giving you."* Ephesians 5:22 says, *"Wives, submit to your own husbands, as to the Lord."* And later in Ephesians 5:25 it says, *"Husbands, love your wives, as Christ loved the church and gave himself*

up for her." Proverbs 17:6 says, *"Grandchildren are the crown of the aged, and the glory of children is their fathers."* 1 Timothy 5:8 says, *"But if anyone does not provide for his relatives, and especially for members of his household, he has denied the faith and is worse than an unbeliever."* And Leviticus 25:35 says, *"If your brother becomes poor and cannot maintain himself with you, you shall support him as though he were a stranger and a sojourner, and he shall live with you."* God clearly values the family unit.

The commands of Scripture are not suggestions based on how your family has treated you in the past. They are loving commands from your Lord who has the absolute best plan in store for you behind every word. God knows that there are wounds from your family. He knows that loving them can be difficult, especially when your love isn't reciprocated. But he is calling you to a lifestyle of grace-filled love for those he has specifically given to you. He will provide for you all the courage, strength, power, and grace you need. He longs to help you love your family into restoration. Have patience with them. Pray constantly for them. And love them as your Lord Jesus has loved you: passionately, faithfully, and gracefully.

93

GUIDED PRAYER

1. Meditate on God's command to love your family. Allow Scripture to influence the way you view the importance of loving your family.

"Honor your father and your mother, that your days may be long in the land that the Lord your God is giving you." Exodus 20:12

"Wives, submit to your own husbands, as to the Lord. For the husband is the head of the wife even as Christ is the head of the church, his body, and is himself its Savior. Now as the church submits to Christ, so also wives should submit in everything to their husbands. Husbands, love your wives, as Christ loved the church and gave himself up for her, that he might sanctify her, having cleansed her by the washing of water with the word, so that he might present the church to himself in splendor, without spot or wrinkle or any such thing, that she might be holy and without blemish. In the same way husbands should love their wives as their own bodies. He who loves his wife loves himself. For no one ever hated his own flesh, but nourishes and cherishes it, just as Christ does the church." Ephesians 5:22-29

"If your brother becomes poor and cannot maintain himself with you, you shall support him as though he were a stranger and a sojourner, and he shall live with you. Take no interest from him or profit, but fear your God, that your brother may live beside you. You shall not lend him your money at interest, nor give him your food for profit. I am the Lord your God, who brought you out of the land of Egypt to give you the land of Canaan, and to be your God." Leviticus 25:35-38

2. Pray for your family. Pray for each family member specifically, and ask God to meet and bless them. As you pray for them, allow the Lord to fill you with grace and love. Allow God to fill you with the knowledge of how he feels about them.

"Praying at all times in the Spirit, with all prayer and supplication. To that end keep alert with all perseverance, making supplication for all the saints . . . " Ephesians 6:18

3. Ask God to empower you to love your family well today. Ask him to give you a creative way to love them. Pursue forgiveness in your own heart as well as with your family. God will help you do what you have felt is impossible. He will fill you with the strength to love your family well.

"I can do all things through him who strengthens me." Philippians 4:13

As you grow in your pursuit of loving your family well, look to Jesus as your model. He loved all those around him perfectly. Sometimes he would speak the truth in love. Other times he would rest with those who simply needed to be around him. Other times he would provide for their physical needs. The Holy Spirit will give you wisdom into exactly how to love your family if you will open your heart and ask him for it. May your family be blessed by the love of God working through you today.

Extended Reading: Ephesians 5

Loving Friends

DEVOTIONAL

Good friends are one of God's greatest gifts. Not one of us is meant to go through life alone and without help. God longs to use you as his hands and feet to those he has placed in your midst. He longs to make you a friend as he is a friend to us, in order to bless others and extend the reach of his kingdom.

*"A friend loves at all times, and a
brother is born for adversity."*

PROVERBS 17:17

1 Samuel 18:1-3 tells of the powerful friendship of David and Jonathan. Scripture says, *"As soon as he had finished speaking to Saul, the soul of Jonathan was knit to the soul of David, and Jonathan loved him as his own soul. And Saul took him that day and would not let him return to his father's house. Then Jonathan made a covenant with David, because he loved him as his own soul."*

Jonathan was an incredible example of God's heart for friendship. Jonathan was the rightful heir to the throne of Israel. Behind Saul's pursuit of killing David was his desire to make Jonathan king. But instead of seeking earthly success, Jonathan humbled himself before David and served him, thereby serving his heavenly Father as well. Jonathan chose friendship over worldly power. As a result, David became Israel's greatest king and ushered in the lineage of Christ.

Proverbs 17:17 says, *"A friend loves at all times, and a brother is born for adversity."* God longs to transform you into a friend who loves others unconditionally. It's in the hard times that we most need our friends. Yet in the hard times, many friends abandon us for relationships that require less of them. The heart of God is to stick with us through trials, sin, and bad decisions. He never leaves us or forsakes us, and he longs to make us like him. He longs to make us friends that will love through every season of life. He longs to empower us to love, serve, honor, and bless those he has intentionally given us.

God is calling you to love your friends *"at all times."* He is calling you to a lifestyle of service and grace. What friend of yours needs your help right now? Who can you choose to serve over yourself? What friend is God calling you to love with the love he has shown you today?

1 Corinthians 13:7 says, *"Love bears all things, believes all things, hopes all things, endures all things."* May you exhibit the heart of your heavenly Father to your friends by loving them as he has loved you.

GUIDED PRAYER

1. Meditate on God's desire for you to pursue godly friendship. Allow Scripture to stir up your desire to love friends well today.

"As soon as he had finished speaking to Saul, the soul of Jonathan was knit to the soul of David, and Jonathan loved him as his own soul. And Saul took him that day and would not let him return to his father's house. Then Jonathan made a covenant with David, because he loved him as his own soul." 1 Samuel 18:1-3

"A friend loves at all times, and a brother is born for adversity." Proverbs 17:17

"A man of many companions may come to ruin, but there is a friend who sticks closer than a brother." Proverbs 18:24

2. How can you be a better friend today? In what ways can you love those God has given you as friends? Ask the Holy Spirit to show you ways you can better love those around you today.

3. Ask God to empower you to be a friend who loves unconditionally. Ask him to make you like himself. Spend time resting in his presence and allowing his love to fill you and empower you.

"So we have come to know and to believe the love that God has for us. God is love, and whoever abides in love abides in God, and God abides in him." 1 John 4:16

Living sacrificially without the burden of entitlement and self-satisfaction is absolutely the most peaceful and joyful way to live. You deserve nothing from others. Christ, Lord of all who deserved everything, sacrificed his life to the point of death for the very people who shouted, *"Crucify him!"* (Luke 23:21). If he pursued love over what was owed him, you are called to do the same. Choose to follow the example of Jesus and love others around you well today. If you do, you will discover a wellspring of abundant life directly connected to the heart of your heavenly Father.

Extended Reading: 1 Samuel 20

Loving Strangers

DAY 20

DEVOTIONAL

Matthew 25:34-40 gives insight into God's passionate love for the lost, broken, and alienated. Scripture says,

Then the King will say to those on his right, 'Come, you who are blessed by my Father, inherit the kingdom prepared for you from the foundation of the world. For I was hungry and you gave me food, I was thirsty and you gave me drink, I was a stranger and you welcomed me, I was naked and you clothed me, I was sick and you visited me, I was in prison and you came to me.' Then the righteous will answer him, saying, 'Lord, when did we see you hungry and feed you, or thirsty and give you drink? And when did we see you a stranger and welcome you, or naked and clothe you? And when did we see you sick or in prison and visit you?' And the King will answer them, 'Truly, I say to you, as you did it to one of the least of these my brothers, you did it to me.'

The world around you is living every day apart from the saving and freeing knowledge of God's love for them. They try to find hope in the created rather than the Creator and discover that the world contains nothing to help them. Relationship with Jesus is the sole source of hope for the earth. And God longs to use us to love the strangers around us so that they might enter into relationship with our Lord who longs to sustain them, provide for them, help them, and offer them eternal hope.

I am not by nature an outgoing person. The concept of talking to complete strangers scares me to death. Apart from God, my natural propensity is to go from place to place without interacting with anyone. But that is not the life my heavenly Father is calling me to. We are not called to keep this free gift of salvation for ourselves, but to share it with all those God is beckoning to himself. God longs to fill each of us with the courage to love the unloved. He longs to fill us with passion to see the world around us awakened to the goodness of Jesus. Every time we set foot outside our homes, we are entering into a mission field filled with countless people who need what we have to give.

Galatians 5:14 says, *"For the whole law is fulfilled in one word: 'You shall love your neighbor as yourself.'"* You were created to receive the love of your Father and go out to share that love with a lost and dying world. God is calling you to a lifestyle of sacrifice, courage, adventure, and passionate pursuit of lost sheep who desperately need a Shepherd.

Allow God to strengthen you and fill you with courage to love strangers today as you enter into a time of guided prayer.

GUIDED PRAYER

1. Meditate on God's command to love your neighbor as yourself. Allow God to fill you with a desire to reach the unreached today as you reflect on his word.

"For the whole law is fulfilled in one word: 'You shall love your neighbor as yourself.'" Galatians 5:14

"Then the King will say to those on his right, 'Come, you who are blessed by my Father, inherit the kingdom prepared for you from the foundation of the world. For I was hungry and you gave me food, I was thirsty and you gave me drink, I was a stranger and you welcomed me, I was naked and you clothed me, I was sick and you visited me, I was in prison and you came to me.' Then the righteous will answer him, saying, 'Lord, when did we see you hungry and feed you, or thirsty and give you drink? And when did we see you a stranger and welcome you, or naked and clothe you? And when did we see you sick or in prison and visit you?' And the King will answer them, 'Truly, I say to you, as you did it to one of the least of these my brothers, you did it to me.'" Matthew 25:34-40

2. What fear holds you back from loving others? What thought, perspective, or past experience does God need to address and speak truth and love to in order for you to effectively love others? Allow him to come and meet with you in the deepest places of your heart.

3. Ask God to fill you with courage to engage with others today. Ask him to fill you with his love for those around you whom you have never met. Find your source of security in his opinion alone.

Luke 10:2 says, *"The harvest is plentiful, but the laborers are few. Therefore pray earnestly to the Lord of the harvest to send out laborers into his harvest."* May we be laborers who work diligently for our Lord today. May we love others with the depth of love we have been shown in Christ.

Extended Reading: Luke 15

Loving
the Church

DAY 21

DEVOTIONAL

The words of Jesus in Matthew 6:9 radically changed the way God's people are to relate to him. Scripture says, *"Pray then like this: 'Our Father in heaven, hallowed by your name.'"* Through Jesus, we now come before God as his child. And because God is our Father, fellow believers are now our

"By this all people will know
that you are my disciples, if you
have love for one another."

JOHN 13:35

spiritual family. Other disciples of Jesus are our brothers and sisters. And church is now a spiritual family reunion designed to be centered around the love and goodness of our Father.

1 John 3:1 says, *"See what kind of love the Father has given to us, that we should be called children of God; and so we are."* We have been brought into fellowship with one another because God loves us. We are children of God because he longs to have the relationship of a father and his children with us. In fact, God created the family unit to be an earthly reflection of God's heavenly family.

And Scripture is clear that it is incredibly important that God's children love one another. Colossians 3:12-15 says, *"Put on then, as God's chosen ones, holy and beloved, compassionate hearts, kindness, humility, meekness, and patience, bearing with one another and, if one has a complaint against another, forgiving each other; as the Lord has forgiven you, so you also must forgive. And above all these put on love, which binds everything together in perfect harmony. And let the peace of Christ rule in your hearts, to which indeed you were called in one body."*

For the church to work as *"one body,"* its members must commit to loving one another as Christ has loved us. Church requires selfless acts of grace, love, honor, and respect. It requires sacrificial commitment. But the result is a glorious union founded on and fueled by the depth of God's love.

And the world will come to join our family as we increasingly love one another. Jesus said in John 13:35, *"By this all people will know that you are my disciples, if you have love for one another."* The world isn't enticed by rules and regulations. And it assuredly isn't enticed with drama, quarreling, bickering, slander, and division. The world needs real, loving relationship with God and his family. The world needs love.

May you be a child of God committed to the people of God. May you receive and give the grace of your heavenly Father to all those he has brought into your spiritual family. And may you love your brothers and sisters in Christ so that the world might know the love of the Father when it sees you. Allow God to fill and empower you to love the church well as you enter into guided prayer.

GUIDED PRAYER

1. Meditate on God's desire for you to sacrificially love the church.

"And above all these put on love, which binds everything together in perfect harmony. And let the peace of Christ rule in your hearts, to which indeed you were called in one body." Colossians 3:14-15

"Love one another with brotherly affection. Outdo one another in showing honor." Romans 12:10

"I do not ask for these only, but also for those who will believe in me through their word, that they may all be one, just as you, Father, are in me, and I in you, that they also may be in us, so that the world may believe that you have sent me." John 17:20-21

2. Reflect on your heart for the church. Allow God to fill you with a greater desire to love others in the family of God. Repent for any ways in which you have made church about anything other than loving God and his children.

3. Ask God to empower you to sacrificially love others in your church. Ask him to fill you with grace and love for his children. Spend time resting in his presence and taking note of his heart for his people. Allow his heart for the church to become your heart.

"So then you are no longer strangers and aliens, but you are fellow citizens with the saints and members of the household of God, built on the foundation of the apostles and prophets, Christ Jesus himself being the

cornerstone, in whom the whole structure, being joined together, grows into a holy temple in the Lord. In him you also are being built together into a dwelling place for God by the Spirit."
Ephesians 2:19-22

God has placed within you a love that can change the trajectory of human lives. May loving others increasingly become a natural extension of your relationship with God. May you be filled with his heart for others daily as you spend time with him. And may he use you in powerful ways to bring his kingdom to earth everywhere you go.

Extended Reading: John 13

Love in action

WEEK

"By this all people will know that you are my disciples, if you have love for one another." John 13:35

WEEKLY OVERVIEW

James 2:26 tells us, *"Faith apart from works is dead."*
If we are going to experience the fullness of life
offered to us through our faith we must be those
who put our words into action. We must not profess
to love God on Sundays and live as if he isn't present,
real, or good on Monday. May your faith come alive
this week as you seek to be a doer of the word.

Action
Fueled by Love

DEVOTIONAL

God has designed the Christian life to be one filled with adventurous and redemptive action—action that is fueled by the love and work of Jesus in our own lives. So great is God's love for us that he would leave the glory of heaven, take on flesh, and destroy the power of sin and death with his loving sacrifice. God's love was so great that he gave himself up for us who are undeserving and could never repay him. And he longs for his love to be the foundation for all we do, think and feel.

As Christians we are to reflect the love we've been shown in Christ through the way we offer compassion and love to those around us. God has appointed us as the sole carriers of his message of redemption for all. He longs to use you to share and exemplify the hope that comes solely through relationship with him. Love doesn't mean all that much just as an idea. The power of God's love comes through action. It comes through helping a stranger, showing compassion and mercy to those who wrong you, serving someone

"For as the body apart from the spirit is dead,
so also faith apart from works is dead."

while expecting nothing in return, and sharing the hope of Christ through word and deed. Jesus proved that love isn't just an idea. Love does.

Bob Goff champions the cause for putting action to love in his book, Love Does. In it he writes, "He says to ordinary people like me and you that instead of closing our eyes and bowing our heads, sometimes God wants us to keep our eyes open for people in need, do something about it, and bow our whole lives to Him instead." In his book he articulates an important spiritual principle—your faith was never intended to be limited to hearing. Your faith was never intended to be limited to conversation. James 2:18 tells us, *"But someone will say, 'You have faith and I have works.' Show me your faith apart from your works, and I will show you my faith by my works."*

What does your love mean if it isn't demonstrated? What would the love of God have meant if he stayed in heaven and never suffered for us? How would you feel about God if he could have saved all of humanity but didn't? Jesus would have been completely justified to stay on his throne. God would have been completely justified to wipe out humanity and start over every time we chose idols over him. But instead he put action to his love for us. He committed the most incredible act of love possible in sending his

Son to die for you and me. Jesus didn't just talk about love. His love was demonstrated in every crack of the whip on his back, in every taunting word, in every nail that pierced his body and in every excruciating gasp for air in which he prayed for us rather than end the torture. He lived out his love for you and me, and he calls us to do the same. 1 John 4:9-11 says,

In this the love of God was made manifest among us, that God sent his only Son into the world, so that we might live through him. In this is love, not that we have loved God but that he loved us and sent his Son to be the propitiation for our sins. Beloved, if God so loved us, we also ought to love one another.

Spend time with God today asking him how you can put your faith into action. In what ways has the love of God been demonstrated to you? In what ways can you share with those around you the incredible gift that's been given to you? Oftentimes, we think of the big things: leading someone to Jesus or selling everything we have. But putting your faith into works could be as simple as a phone call, a cooked meal, a kind word, or a hug. Whatever God shows you, choose to live life as a believer whose faith and works are tethered, bringing redemption to a world desperately in need of God's grace.

GUIDED PRAYER

1. Take a minute to meditate on God's love put into action. Choose to make Jesus your example.

"In this the love of God was made manifest among us, that God sent his only Son into the world, so that we might live through him. In this is love, not that we have loved God but that he loved us and sent his Son to be the propitiation for our sins. Beloved, if God so loved us, we also ought to love one another." 1 John 4:9-11

2. Now ask God how he would have you put action to love today. What can you do to show the Father's love to those around you?

"For as the body apart from the spirit is dead, so also faith apart from works is dead." James 2:26

3. Ask the Spirit to fill you with the strength and courage to do the works he has planned for you today in love. Let him empower you with his presence.

The Holy Spirit longs to help you connect with God and live out of the fruit of your relationship. He longs to empower you to love others. By his power and grace you can do incredible, eternal and impactful things with your time on earth. You are the child of God, made in his image and filled with same Spirit that raised Christ from the dead. Lean on God, ask for his help and have the courage to submit to his leadership today.

Extended Reading: James 2

Love is Present

DAY 23

DEVOTIONAL

One of the most comforting aspects of God's character is that he is present. Jesus made clear God's desire to be present when he left his throne and took on humanity. God has never desired distance with his children. He fights to have close relationship with us every day. This week we're

"Where shall I go from your Spirit? Or where shall I flee from your presence?"

119

looking at how we can not only receive God's word, but experience more of God through being doers of his word. So, today let's explore how we can follow the example of Jesus and be present for those around us.

Being present in people's lives always requires sacrifice. It requires stepping outside of what will solely benefit you in order to live for the benefit of others. Philippians 2:3 teaches us, *"Do nothing from selfish ambition or conceit, but in humility count others more significant than yourselves."* Jesus counted you and me as more significant than his own life. He died so that we might live, and he calls us to do the same. Luke 9:23 says, *"If anyone would come after me, let him deny himself and take up his cross daily and follow me."* John 12:24 makes it clear that in order to bear fruit in this life we must die to ourselves: *"Truly, truly, I say to you, unless a grain of wheat falls into the earth and dies, it remains alone; but if it dies, it bears much fruit."* Choose today to be a doer of the word, and die to yourself that you might better love others.

You see, before people need your advice they need your presence. Before our need to be fixed we simply need to know we are loved and cared for. It's in the giving and receiving of love that healing takes place. Being present creates space for them to thrive, heal and be transformed.

Who in your life needs you to be present for them today? In what ways has God been present in your own life? In what ways has he demonstrated his nearness to you? And in what ways could you be his reflection today? I promise you there is someone around you that just needs you to be present in their life. There is someone who simply needs to know that somebody would love them enough to think about them—to be near to them. Take time today to let someone know you are there for them. Listen, love, and watch as God works through you simply being present in the lives of others.

GUIDED PRAYER

1. Take a moment to reflect on God's nearness to you. Receive his presence. Encounter his closeness.

"Where shall I go from your Spirit? Or where shall I flee from your presence? If I ascend to heaven, you are there! If I make my bed in Sheol, you are there! If I take the wings of the morning and dwell in the uttermost parts of the sea, even there your hand shall lead me, and your right hand shall hold me. If I say, 'Surely the darkness shall cover me, and the light about me be night,' even the darkness is not dark to you; the night is bright as the day, for darkness is as light with you." Psalm 139:7-12

2. Now ask the Spirit to show you someone who needs you to be present for them today. Spend some time thinking about and praying for that person.

3. Ask God how he would have you be present in their life. How can you be a reflection of God's love to them today?

Have the courage to humble yourself before people around you. Count them as more significant than yourself. You being present isn't about what they can give you in return or even how they appear to receive your love. Love selflessly today the way Jesus did, and experience the joy and peace that comes from serving rather than seeking to be served.

Extended Reading: Psalm 139

Love Makes
Time for Others

DAY 24

SCRIPTURE

"Now when Jesus returned, the crowd welcomed him, for they were all waiting for him. And there came a man named Jairus, who was a ruler of the synagogue. And falling at Jesus' feet, he implored him to come to his house, for he had an only daughter, about twelve years of age, and she was dying." Luke 8:40-42

DEVOTIONAL

There's a story in Luke 8:40-42, 49-56 that gives us insight into Jesus's love for those in need. Luke writes,

Now when Jesus returned, the crowd welcomed him, for they were all waiting for him. And there came a man named Jairus, who was a ruler of the synagogue. And falling at Jesus' feet, he implored him to come to his house, for he had an only daughter, about twelve years of age, and she was dying. . . While he was still speaking, someone from the ruler's house came and said, "Your daughter is dead; do not trouble the Teacher any more." But Jesus on hearing this answered him, "Do not fear; only believe, and she will be well." And when he came to the house, he allowed no one to enter with him, except Peter and John and James, and the father and mother of the child. And all were weeping and mourning for her, but he said, "Do not weep, for she is not dead but sleeping." And they laughed at him, knowing that she was dead. But taking her by the hand he called, saying, "Child, arise." And her spirit returned, and she got up at once. And he directed that something should be given her to eat. And her parents were amazed, but he charged them to tell no one what had happened.

Jesus made time for those in need. He wasn't too busy to leave what he was doing, which happened to be ministering to a large group of people, to make time for a single girl. Jesus displayed the heart of the Father in going after the one. Throughout his ministry, Jesus consistently made time for people around him. Whether it was eating a meal with his disciples, going to the house of Zacchaeus, or spending time with little children, Jesus was there for those around him.

God is the same way with you and me today. Through the death of Jesus we have been given an opportunity to have conversation with God all day, every day. God's desire is to make time for us. He counts our needs as important. Jesus's ministry exemplified God's heart to make time for his children.

This week as we are looking at what it means to not only be a hearer of God's word but a doer, let's ask God how we could be more like Jesus. In what ways could you make time for those around you today? Will you choose to spend time with someone in need even if it doesn't fit in your schedule? Will you put those around you above yourself? If you will choose to be a doer of God's word today, you will experience the joy of not living just for your own goals and pursuits, but for the benefit of others around you. Spend some time with God in prayer today, and ask him to help you know when and how to make time for those around you in need.

GUIDED PRAYER

1. Reflect on Jesus's heart to make time for those in need. Choose to make Jesus your example.

"While he was still speaking, someone from the ruler's house came and said, 'Your daughter is dead; do not trouble the Teacher any more.' But Jesus on hearing this answered him, 'Do not fear; only believe, and she will be well.' And when he came to the house, he allowed no one to enter with him, except Peter and John and James, and the father and mother of the child." Luke 8:49-51

2. Who needs you to make time for them? Ask God to bring someone to mind you can love well today.

3. How can you spend time with someone in need today? How could you make time to listen to, help, or simply be there for someone?

Love is powerful. It has the power to lead someone to Jesus, heal a wounded heart, and even help someone on the path to restored relationship with God. It's worth your effort to make time for those around you today. Jesus never wasted a minute. He did everything in perfect accordance with the Father's will. You won't be missing out if you make time for someone today. Follow the leadership of the Holy Spirit as you seek to love others well.

Extended Reading: Luke 19

Love
Encourages

DEVOTIONAL

When was the last time someone really encouraged you? Maybe it was a family member or friend. How did it make you feel? How did you view yourself afterwards? If you haven't been encouraged in a while, how greatly do you long for it?

Encouragement is powerful! It has the ability to change emotions and trajectories. It has the power to fill someone with courage and boldness to say yes to the plans and heart of God. Encouragement is truly a gift we've been given for edifying each other. We are meant to encourage one another. The Bible makes

it clear that as brothers and sisters in Christ, we are meant to both give and receive encouragement. Hebrews 10:23-25 says, *"Let us hold fast the confession of our hope without wavering, for he who promised is faithful. And let us consider how to stir up one another to love and good works, not neglecting to meet together, as is the habit of some, but encouraging one another, and all the more as you see the Day drawing near."*

Have you ever thought about how you could change the day of a complete stranger just with a few kind words? Jesus knew the power of encouragement.

> *"Let us hold fast the confession of our hope without waver-ing, for he who promised is faithful. And let us consider how to stir up one another to love and good works, not neglecting to meet together, as is the habit of some, but encouraging one another, and all the more as you see the Day drawing near."*

HEBREWS 10:23-25

He loved to use the tool of encouragement to direct his disciples into the life God intended for them. Jesus spoke life into the people he encountered. He encouraged the outcasts, the downhearted, the needy. A perfect example of the power of encouragement can be found in the story of Zacchaeus. Luke 19:1-10 reads,

He entered Jericho and was passing through. And behold, there was a man named Zacchaeus. He was a chief tax collector and was rich. And he was seeking to see who Jesus was, but on account of the crowd he could not, because he was small in stature. So he ran on ahead and climbed up into a sycamore tree to see him, for he was about to pass that way. And when Jesus came to the place, he looked up and said to him, "Zacchaeus, hurry and come down, for I must stay at your house today." So he hurried and came down and received him joyfully. And when they saw it, they all grumbled, "He has gone in to be the guest of a man who is a sinner." And Zacchaeus stood and said to the Lord, "Behold, Lord, the half of my goods I give to the poor. And if I have defrauded anyone of anything, I restore it fourfold." And Jesus said to him, "Today salvation has come to this house, since he also is a son of Abraham. For the Son of Man came to seek and to save the lost."

Jesus encouraged an outcast tax collector and changed the trajectory of his life. He simply told Zacchaeus that he wanted to spend time with him, followed through with that commitment, and the entire town was blessed. Zacchaeus got his income through overtaxing his own people for the benefit of Rome and himself. He was cast out from society and hated by those around him. Jesus, to the dismay of the others, encouraged Zacchaeus, spent time with him, and changed his life.

You can live like Jesus today. Who needs an encouraging word from you? Who needs to be encouraged by you simply wanting to spend some time with them? There's grace on your life to minister to the hurting and lonely around you. There's grace to minister like Jesus. Walk in relationship with your heavenly Father, live with the knowledge that you are fully loved, and love others through the power of encouragement.

GUIDED PRAYER

1. Take some time to meditate on what the Bible says about encouragement.

"Therefore encourage one another and build one another up, just as you are doing." 1 Thessalonians 5:11

"Let no corrupting talk come out of your mouths, but only such as is good for building up, as fits the occasion, that it may give grace to those who hear." Ephesians 4:29

"Anxiety in a man's heart weighs him down, but a good word makes him glad." Proverbs 12:25

2. Ask the Lord whom he would have you encourage today. Maybe it's a co-worker that's seemed down lately, a family member going through a hard time or even a stranger that just needs a kind word.

3. Ask God how he would have you encourage that person. It could be as simple as sending a text message or taking someone out for a meal. Maybe it's a few kind words or help financially. Ask the Spirit to help you follow his leadership.

The Bible makes it clear that the tongue wields incredible power. Proverbs 18:21 says, *"Death and life are in the power of the tongue, and those who love it will eat its fruits."* Choose to speak life today. Choose to honor those around you instead of condemn. Choose to see the grace God has placed in people around you—to see past the façade and tough exterior people put up and speak to the heart. God intends for you to both give and receive encouragement. Who will you speak life into today?

Extended Reading: Romans 12

Love Forgives

DAY 26

DEVOTIONAL

We're promised forgiveness from our Father because his forgiveness is offered in complete grace. Ephesians 1:7 says, *"In [Jesus] we have redemption through his blood, the forgiveness of our trespasses, according to the riches of his grace."* We have done nothing to deserve the forgiveness God so freely lavishes upon us. God offers us forgiveness because he is love; it is his very nature. And as Jesus demonstrated through his death, love forgives.

Sin stood between us and God like a great chasm separating a wanderer from an oasis; and so great was the Father's love for us that he sent his only Son that we might be justly forgiven. Jesus fully bore the weight of

our sin. In doing so, he received the wrath of God on our behalf that we might be afforded restored relationship with our heavenly Father. He set aside what was fair for himself and chose to give grace. *"For our sake he made him to be sin who knew no sin, so that in him we might become the righteousness of God"* (2 Corinthians 5:21).

Christianity is the only religion where salvation is based on grace instead of works. God, in his love, has laid before us a path founded on mercy, and he calls us to do the same for others. As the children of God, brought into his family solely by his grace, we must forgive as God has forgiven us. Colossians 3:13 says, *"[Bear] with one another and, if one has a complaint against another,*

*"Be kind to one another, tenderheart-
ed, forgiving one another, as God in
Christ forgave you."*

EPHESIANS 4:32

[forgive] each other; as the Lord has forgiven you, so you also must forgive." Jesus modeled forgiveness perfectly in laying down his own life for you and me. In order for us to forgive others, we must be like Jesus and die to our own rights for the sake of the person who has wronged us. Forgiveness requires humility. It is a decision to offer unmerited grace because *"as the Lord has forgiven you, so you also must forgive."*

Think about your own life for a moment. Who in your life do you feel has wronged you? It could be a small wound. It could be a life-altering sin committed against you. Maybe a parent left you. Maybe you were abused. Maybe you lost a job opportunity that should have been yours. Maybe it was a word someone spoke against you that hurt you. Whatever sin was committed against you, large or small, call it back to mind. Feel the injustice over it.

Now reflect for a minute on the sin of the world committed against God. The story of humanity is a fall from perfection because of pride. In every age thus far, man has chosen his own way over God's and has thereby perpetuated the cycle of sin and destruction we live in today. God placed his judgement over the sins of all humanity, past and present, on the person of Jesus because he couldn't take being separated from you and me. We have all been wronged, but no one more than God. Every day humanity turns away from God.

God weeps over what's been done to you. He knows your pain because people wrong him every minute of every day. But still he chooses to forgive because there is no love without forgiveness. There is no abundant life apart from restoration of relationship. There is no joy for God or us when we harden our hearts and live for what is fair rather than what is good.

We aren't called to forgive because someone deserves it. We forgive because love requires it. We forgive because abundant life requires it. Choose love today over your own sense of fairness. Choose to be like your heavenly Father and forgive those who have wronged you. Choose to be a doer of Colossians 3:13 and *"[forgive] each other; as the Lord has forgiven you, so you also must forgive."* You weren't made to live with the weight of unforgiveness, so don't bear it any longer. The Spirit will help you. He will give you the strength and courage to do what seems impossible. Spend some time in God's presence today and forgive as he guides and directs you.

131

GUIDED PRAYER

1. Meditate on God's heart to forgive. Allow God's forgiveness to be the foundation for your own.

"As far as the east is from the west, so far does he remove our transgressions from us." Psalm 103:12

"Gracious is the Lord, and righteous; our God is merciful. The Lord preserves the simple; when I was brought low, he saved me. Return, O my soul, to your rest; for the Lord has dealt bountifully with you." Psalm 116:5-7

2. Ask the Spirit who you need to forgive. Whether the wound was small or big, to whom do you need to offer grace today?

3. Forgive that person. Forgive them in your heart right now. If you can, set up a meeting with them to talk through what happened. The awkwardness or pain of the conversation will never outweigh the lasting peace you will experience from offering grace and forgiveness.

"[Bear] with one another and, if one has a complaint against another, [forgive] each other; as the Lord has forgiven you, so you also must forgive." Colossians 3:13

Forgiveness is a process. But it is a process worth going through. Assess your heart immediately after you've been wronged. Go through the process of forgiveness instead of allowing the wound to be reopened time and time again. The French proverb says, *"Write injuries in sand, kindnesses in marble."* It's ok to be hurt. It's only harmful if you write your wounds in marble and let them linger longer than they should. God has designed you in his image and has given you his Spirit. You have the strength to forgive. So choose love today and every day. Allow the Spirit to work in your heart, healing the wounds people and life have caused you through the wonderful gift of forgiveness.

Extended Reading: Colossians 3

Love Hopes

DAY 27

DEVOTIONAL

Through Jesus we have been afforded an anchor of hope. Through God's promises of his presence now and total restoration in the age to come, we can have peace in the midst of trials, joy in persecution and steadfastness when it seems nothing can go our way. 1 Peter 1:3-4 says, *"Blessed be the God and Father of our Lord Jesus Christ! According to his*

*"Love bears all things, believes all things,
hopes all things, endures all things."*

135

great mercy, he has caused us to be born again to a living hope through the resurrection of Jesus Christ from the dead, to an inheritance that is imperishable, undefiled, and unfading, kept in heaven for you." As believers, we have an inheritance of boundless communion with our heavenly Father. And with this inheritance we are called to share our hope with a lost and hopeless world.

The hope that's been freely given to you was not meant to be solely contained within you. You have a testimony in Christ that has the power to transform lives. 1 Corinthians 13:7 says, *"Love bears all things, believes all things, hopes all things, endures all things."* You are called to hope for a better life for those around you. You are called to believe in people when no one else will. God has abundant life and relationship for all if they will simply come to know him. And he's chosen to use his children to share that message of hope. Your life has been transformed from being lost and lifeless to being filled with the powerful hope of

the gospel. No one is hopeless. No one is beyond the saving grace of Jesus. And God is calling you to love others enough to share with them the reality of his love in both word and deed that they might have hope in God.

The only hope the world has is Jesus. No amount of money, no friends, and no politician can save us from the destruction of sin. The truth of God's unconditional love and unmerited grace is the only source of redemption and joy this world has.

So who around you needs hope today? Who around you needs to know that God has a plan for their life? Who around you needs you to have hope in *"all things"* for them today? There is no love without hope. There is no gospel without hope. In you lies the hope for all the world, the message of salvation through Jesus Christ. Share that hope with those around you today who are in desperate need of restored relationship with their heavenly Father.

GUIDED PRAYER

1. Reflect on the hope you have in Jesus. Allow Scripture to remind you of the destruction that awaited you apart from God's saving grace.

"Blessed be the God and Father of our Lord Jesus Christ! According to his great mercy, he has caused us to be born again to a living hope through the resurrection of Jesus Christ from the dead, to an inheritance that is imperishable, undefiled, and unfading, kept in heaven for you." 1 Peter 1:3-4

"Whoever believes and is baptized will be saved, but whoever does not believe will be condemned." Mark 16:16

2. Ask God who he would have you hope *"in all things"* for today. Who around you needs someone who will simply believe in them and reflect the unconditional love of God?

3. Ask the Spirit to show you how you can share the message of hope with that person today. How can you reveal God's heart of grace, love and peace?

Both believers and non-believers need hope. Everyone needs love from the people around them. Whether you're sharing the gospel with someone for the first time or helping a fellow believer through a tough time, you are needed by the people around you. Exemplify the hope God offers as Jesus did, and watch as lives are transformed around you. May your day be filled with reconciliation and good works as you allow the Holy Spirit to use you.

Extended Reading: Romans 5

Love Wins

SCRIPTURE

"No, in all these things we are more than conquerors through him who loved us. For I am sure that neither death nor life, nor angels nor rulers, nor things present nor things to come, nor powers, nor height nor depth, nor anything else in all creation, will be able to separate us from the love of God in Christ Jesus our Lord." Romans 8:37-39

DEVOTIONAL

Through Jesus, God has obtained victory in the earth. The dominion the devil had over humanity was crushed by the cross of Jesus Christ. Colossians 2:13-15 says, *"And you, who were dead in your trespasses and the uncircumcision of your flesh, God made alive together with him, having forgiven us all our trespasses, by canceling the record of debt that stood against us with its legal demands. This he set aside, nailing it to the cross. He disarmed the rulers and authorities and put them to open shame, by triumphing over them in him."* Jesus has triumphed over everything that stood between us and a life lived in relationship with God.

One of my favorite chapters in all of Scripture, Romans 8, tells us, *"No, in all these things we are more than conquerors through him who loved us. For I am sure that neither death nor life, nor angels nor rulers, nor things present nor things to come, nor powers, nor height nor depth, nor anything else in all creation, will be able to separate us from the love of God in Christ Jesus our Lord"* (Romans 8:37-39). We've been given victory over the enemy and all his schemes. But even though we have obtained victory in Jesus, the devil still works to lead you and me back into our former ways. Even though Jesus has defeated the enemy, we still must live out that victory every day and help others around us do the same. Even though love has won, we still must fight for the victory in others.

We need each other to experience the freedom available to us in Christ. Scripture admonishes us to engage in confession, community, worship, and spiritual battle together. Proverbs 27:17 says, *"Iron sharpens iron, and one man sharpens another."* James 5:13-16 says, *"Is anyone among you suffering? Let him pray. Is anyone cheerful? Let him sing praise. Is anyone among you sick? Let him call for the elders of the church, and let them pray over him, anointing him with oil in the name of the Lord. And the prayer of faith will save the one who is sick, and the Lord will raise him up. And if he has committed sins, he will be forgiven. Therefore, confess your sins to one another and pray for one another, that you may be healed. The prayer of a righteous person has great power as it is working."* We must engage with one another and fight for a life lived victoriously in Christ together. The Bible is clear that sanctification is a process worked out, and it's a process meant to be worked out together.

We must call out the greatness in each other. If you see a brother or sister struggling with temptation, fight for them through prayer. Speak life into them. Encourage them in who God has made them to be. Stand with them through whatever circumstances and consequences come their way. See them through the fight until they experience victory over the power of sin and darkness in their life. Open up to those around you and ask for their help in your own life! You don't have to fight spiritual battles alone. There are people around you who will fight for victory in your own life.

Through Christ, love has won. He has paved the way of victory for you and me. We are the world's no longer. Ephesians 2:10 says, *"For we are his workmanship, created in Christ Jesus for good works, which God prepared beforehand, that we should walk in them."* Walk in the works God intends for you today and, in love, fight for those around you to do the same. You and I are meant for more in this life than the struggle with sin. Let's fight for the victory in each other.

GUIDED PRAYER

1. Renew your mind to the victory available to you in Christ.

"And you, who were dead in your trespasses and the uncircumcision of your flesh, God made alive together with him, having forgiven us all our trespasses, by canceling the record of debt that stood against us with its legal demands. This he set aside, nailing it to the cross. He disarmed the rulers and authorities and put them to open shame, by triumphing over them in him." Colossians 2:13-15

2. Who needs you to fight for their victory today.

Who needs encouragement from you? Who needs you to speak truth over them in love? Who needs you to intercede on their behalf?

3. Pray for their victory. However the Spirit prompts you, pray that they would overcome the power of sin in their lives. Trust that God will move when you pray.

"The prayer of a righteous person has great power as it is working." James 5:16

You don't have to be perfect before you can fight for the victory in someone else's life. You don't have to be fully experiencing freedom before your Father would use you to help someone else. If the only people that could engage in ministry had to be perfect, the movement of Christianity would have died long ago. You are equipped to help right now exactly as you are. Engage in community with fellow believers as God intends and experience more life together as you walk in the victory laid out before you by the power of Jesus' death and resurrection.

Extended Reading: 1 Corinthians 15